Natural

Language

Processing

***

A Quick Introduction to NLP
with Python and NLTK

*

Step-by-Step Tutorial for Beginners

Samuel Burns

Please note the information contained within this document is for educational and entertainment purposes only. No warranties of any kind are expressed or implied. Readers acknowledge that the author is not engaging in the rendering of legal, financial, medical or professional advice. Please consult a licensed professional before attempting any techniques outlined in this book.

By reading this document, the reader agrees that under no circumstances is the author responsible for any losses, direct or indirect, which are incurred as a result of the use of the information contained within this document, including, but not limited to, errors, omissions, or inaccuracies.

Natural Language Processing : A Quick Introduction to NLP With Python and NLTK 2nd Edition

Editor: Maria Rica/GlobaltechNTC

Editorial Assistant: Zokolodni Sergey

E-Media Editor: Daniel Soler

Book Design: Rebecca.

Collection : **(Step-by-Step Guide For Beginners)**

Publisher: **Amazon KDP Printing and Publishing**

Contact: **globaltechntc@bk.ru**

ASIN: B07V1F3PYQ

Imprint: Independently published

First Edition: July 2019

CONTENTS

Introduction

Today, a lot of data is available for processing. This data is generated by blogs, social websites and web pages. This data carries a lot of information. However, there is a need for a way that will help businesses transform the data into information. Natural Language Processing is one of such tools. It is a branch of artificial intelligence that deals with machines understanding natural languages such as English. It is through natural language processing that computers can understand human speech.

Companies usually generate data in huge volumes, running up to gigabytes. It may be hard for companies to process such data manually. However, with natural language processing, a computer can be trained to process text written in a natural language and extract information from it. This means that the computer will be able to identify the nouns, verbs, adjectives, punctuation marks, etc. contained in the text. Through natural language processing, we can identify the attitude of the person who wrote a particular text. The computer will able to tell how positive or negative a certain text is. Due to this, businesses have benefited a lot from natural language processing as they can analyze customer feedback on their products to know how positive or negative they are towards their products.

This book is an excellent guide for you to learn natural language processing in detail. The author guides you on how to perform natural language processing tasks in Python programming language. You will also learn how to set up and use the Natural Language Processing Toolkit (NLTK).

1-Getting started with Natural Language Processing

NLP (Natural Language Processing) is a branch of artificial intelligence and computer science that deals with the interactions between computers and human languages. With NLP, machine learning algorithms can be applied to speech and text. With NLP, we develop systems with the ability to understand human languages.

Blogs, social websites, and web pages are generating gigabytes of data every day. There are companies that collect this data for processing so that they can better understand the users better. When such data is processed, companies can gain information about the passions and interests of their customers. This can help them adjust their plans appropriately to meet the demands of users.

With natural language processing, a computer can understand the human language while being spoken. The popularity of natural language processing is rising every day, thanks to the availability of big data, growing interest in machine-human communications and the discovery of new computing algorithms. With natural language processing, an intelligent system such as a robot can perform according to our instructions issued in a plain language such as English.

Syntax and semantic analysis are very important components in NLP. Syntax deals with the arrangement or how words in a sentence are structured to make a grammatical sense. NLP makes use of syntax to analyze to assess the meaning from a language depending on grammatical rules. Some syntax techniques that are used for this include parsing, word segmentation, sentence breaking, morphological segmentation and stemming.

Semantic is associated with the use and the meaning of various words. In NLP, algorithms are used to analyze and determine the meaning and structure of sentences. Some NLP techniques used for semantics include word sense disambiguation, named entity recognition and natural language generation.

Most of the current approaches to NLP are using deep learning. Deep learning is a type of artificial intelligence that relies on the patterns in data to improve the understanding of a program. Deep learning models usually require huge amounts of labeled data to train and identify any correlations between the data elements. However, it becomes hard for one to assemble this huge amount of labeled data.

Initially, NLP approaches involved the use of rule-based approaches, in which simple algorithms were used and given instructions about the phrases and words to look for in a sample of text and given specific responses to be returned when such phrases are found. However, deep learning is a more intuitive and complex approach that involves the use of algorithms to identify the intent of the speaker from numerous examples in the same way that a child learns a language.

In this book, we will explore natural language processing in detail. We will be using NLTK, Natural Language Toolkit which is a Python module with datasets and tutorials. It is an open source library.

To install this library, use pip, a package manager that comes with Python. Just run the following command on the terminal of your operating system:

```
pip3 install nltk
```

In the above case, I have used the pip3 command since I am using Python 3.X.

2-Text wrangling and cleansing

The purpose of doing text processing is to change the text into a format that is easy for machines to read. Text processing is very important as it helps us understand our data better and gain insights from it. Text processing normally involves the following steps:

1. Tokenization
2. Lemmatization
3. Stemming
4. Stopword removal

Before we can begin to process data, we should first load it into our workspace from its source. The data to be loaded can be in various formats including **CSV, HTML, Database, JSON, XML, NoSQL, PDF** etc. There are various ways through which we can parse this data from the source. Some of the Python parsers that we can use for this include import **CSV**, import **HTML** parser, import **json**.

Once the data has been loaded from the source, it is time for us to make sense from the raw data. This is always a challenge. The text obtained from the source has noise. Our goal is to remove all this noise so that we can be able to make sense of the data.

Now that you have the **nltk** installed on your computer, run the code given below from the Python command line:

```
import nltk
nltk.download('punkt')
```

```
>>> import nltk
>>> nltk.download('punkt')
[nltk_data] Downloading package punkt to
[nltk_data]     C:\Users\admin\AppData\Roaming\nltk_data...
[nltk_data]   Unzipping tokenizers\punkt.zip.
True
>>>
```

What we have done is that we have started by importing the **nltk** library. We have then downloaded the *punkt*, which is a *tokenizer* for a text into a list of sentences. We can now do text wrangling.

Sentence Splitting

You must have wanted to analyze a paragraph. You know that the best way to analyze the paragraph and understand it well by splitting it into a set of sentences. Even in real life communications, we analyze the communications at the sentence level in which we analyze the conjoined words.

However, splitting a paragraph into sentences may not be easy as you think, especially with the **raw code**. However, we can easily do this with the **nltk** package.

Run the code given below:

```
from nltk.tokenize import sent_tokenize
myString = "This is a paragraph. It should split
at the end of sentence marker, such as a period.
It can tell that the period in Mr. John is not an
end. Run it!"

tokenized_sentence = sent_tokenize(myString)
print(tokenized_sentence)
```

The code may sound simple to you especially if you have some background in Python. We began by importing *sent_tokenize*, which is a sentence tokenization library provided by the **nltk** library.

After that, we have created a variable and given it the name *myString*. We have assigned a number of sentences to this variable. Note that you are allowed to change these sentences to your own sentences.

We have then called the *sent_tokenize* function that we have imported. We have passed our variable *myString* to this variable. What this does is that it will execute the tokenization on our string and the result of this operation will be saved in the variable *tokenized_sentence*.

Lastly, we have printed the value of the variable *tokenized_sentence* on the console.

Your output should be something related to the following:

```
['This is a paragraph.', 'It should split at the end of sentence marker, such as
a period.', 'It can tell that the period in Mr. John is not an end.', 'Run it!'
]
```

As you can see in the above output, the paragraph was split into the exact sentences. It was also able to tell the difference between a period that has been used to end a sentence from one used on the name **Mr. John.**

T o k e n i z a t i o n

Tokenization refers to the process by which a large text is broken down into various pieces. In NLP, a token is the minimal piece of text that a machine can be able to understand. A text may be tokenized into words or sentences. For the case of sentence tokenization, every sentence will be seen as a token. In word tokenization, every word will be seen as a token.

There are various ways through which tokenization can be done, but the most popular way of doing it is through word tokenization. What happens in word tokenization is that a large text is broken down into words and the words are used as the tokens. The words will then serve as the minimal units. Some modules that can be used for tokenization include:

- word_tokenizer
- sent_tokenizer
- punkt_tokenizer
- Regexp_tokenizer
- TreebankWord_Tokenizer

To tokenize a text, we only need to call the ***split() function*** provided by **nltk.** The following example demonstrates this:

```
from nltk.tokenize import sent_tokenize
myString = "These are sentences. Let us tokenize
it! Run it!"

print(myString.split())
```

```
['These', 'are', 'sentences.', 'Let', 'us', 'tokenize', 'it!', 'Run', 'it!']
```

We created some sentences and assigned them to the variable *myString*. We then called the *split() function* on this variable and printed the results on the console.

The *split() function* provides us with a very simple tokenizer. It uses white space as the delimiter. Its process of tokenization is done based on words, meaning that the word will be the simplest token. There are several other functions that we can use for this and the good news is that they can give us advanced results.

Consider the following example:

```
from nltk.tokenize import word_tokenize,
regexp_tokenize

myString = "These are sentences. Let us tokenize
it! Run it!"
print(word_tokenize(myString))
```

This will return the following result upon execution:

```
['These', 'are', 'sentences', '.', 'Let', 'us', 'tokenize', 'it', '!', 'Run', 'i
t', '!']
```

Note the two functions that we have imported above. We then created the string and called the *word_tokenize() function* on it. The function works in the same way as the *split() function* but with one major difference. The function doesn't rely on the whitespace as the delimiter but even punctuation marks like period and exclamation mark are tokenized.

regex_tokenize is another tokenization function that can return advanced results. It can also be customized to return results which suits one's needs. Let us see how this function works by creating an example:

```
from nltk.tokenize import word_tokenize,
regexp_tokenize

myString = "These are sentences. Let us tokenize
it! Run it!"
print(regexp_tokenize(myString, pattern="\w+"))
```

The code should return the result given below upon execution:

```
['These', 'are', 'sentences', 'Let', 'us', 'tokenize', 'it', 'Run', 'it']
```

Notice the use of an extra parameter in the above function named pattern. This parameter helps developers to choose the way they need to tokenize their text. The **\w+** is an indication that we need all the words and digits to be in the token, but symbols such as punctuation marks can be ignored.

In the above example, we have used the method with the **\w+** pattern. Let us demonstrate how to use the function with another pattern:

```
from nltk.tokenize import word_tokenize,
regexp_tokenize

myString = "These are 3 sentences. Let us
tokenize them! Run the code!"
print(regexp_tokenize(myString, pattern="\d+"))
```

The code will return the following upon execution:

```
['3']
```

We have used the same function but with a different pattern, the **\d+** pattern. This pattern asks the function to return digits only. This explains why our output only has an output of 3. It is the only digit that was found in the string.

Those are the common functions that you need to know as far as text wrangling is concerned.

Stemming

This is another step in text wrangling. From the name, you can get the meaning, cutting down a token to its root stem. Consider the word **"cutting"**. This word can be broken down to its root, which is **"cut"**. However, there could be many variations of the root. For example, for the word **"running"**, the root is **"run"**. This word can have variations such as **ran, runs,** etc. With stemming, it is possible for us to club all the variations of a certain word into a single root.

Consider the sample code given below:

```
from nltk.stem import PorterStemmer
porter = PorterStemmer()
print(porter.stem("cutting"))
```

We began by importing the PorterStemmer function from the toolkit. There are numerous algorithms that can be used for stemming words, and the PorterStemmer uses one of these algorithms. However, it relies on numerous rules, making it the best to use for this.

We have then created a variable and given it the name porter. The value of this variable has been equated to **PorterStemmer(()**.

We have then asked the stemmer to stem the word **"cutting"**. The code should return the following result once executed:

```
cut
```

That is how the above stemmer can be used. Let us discuss other stemmers that use different algorithms. Let us begin with Lancaster Stemming.

Consider the code given below:

```
from nltk.stem import LancasterStemmer
lancaster = LancasterStemmer()
print(lancaster.stem("sleeping"))
```

The code should return the following when executed:

```
sleep
```

In the previous example, we imported the **PorterStemmer** function. In this above example, we have imported the **LancasterStemmer** function.

We have created the variable named **lancaster** and assigned its value to the **LancasterStemmer() function**.

We have then passed the word "sleeping" to it for stemming. The results have been printed on the console.

We also have **SnowballStemmer**. The good thing with this stemmer is that it has been trained in multiple languages and it can work with languages such as English, German, Russian,

French, and others. Its implementation is a bit different from the previous stemmers. Its implementation is discussed below:

```
from nltk.stem.snowball import SnowballStemmer
snowball = SnowballStemmer("english")
print(snowball.stem("driving"))
```

The code returns the following result upon execution:

```
drive
```

Notice how the import has been done in the first line. Instead of doing it from **nltk.stem**, the import has been done from **inltk.stem.snowball**, and we have imported **SnowballStemme**r.

We have then defined our stemmer as a **snowball**. Notice that it is in the same line that we have specified the language, in which case it is the language that the **stemmer** is expected to detect.

We have finally used the created stemmer to stem the word **driving** and print the results on the console.

Stemming is good for its simplicity when it comes to dealing with NLP problems. However, when more complex stemming is needed, stemming is not the best option, but we have **lemmatization.**

Lemmatization

Lemmatization is a more advanced compared to stemming since rather than just following rules, it puts into consideration the context and part of the speech to determine the root of the word, also known as the **lemma**. The example given below shows the difference between stemming and lemmatization:

```
import nltk
from nltk.stem import WordNetLemmatizer
from nltk.stem import PorterStemmer

nltk.download('wordnet')
porter = PorterStemmer()
lemma = WordNetLemmatizer()
print(lemma.lemmatize("drove"))
print(porter.stem("drove"))
```

The code will return the following when executed:

```
drive
drove
```

We started by importing a number of libraries, including the **WordNetLemmatizer** from **nltk.stem**. We started by downloading **wordnet** from the toolkit. A wordnet is a semantic dictionary with massive words from which we can perform search-specific lemmas of words.

We have defined the variable's *porter* and *lemma* and assigned them to the **PorterStemmer** and **WordNetLemmatizer** functions. We have then lemmatized the word drove and printed the results on the console.

The reason we have used both is that we needed to perform a comparison between them. Note that you may not get the above result because **wordnet** is updated regularly. In my case, I got the above result.

The output shows that we lemmatization, it is possible for us to detect the tenses of words and have the word presented in its simplest form. See we have used only a few lines of code to achieve this. This shows that lemmatization is a great technique that we can use for text wrangling.

Stop Word Removal

Stop words are the words that are used commonly and they are normally ignored because of their frequent occurrences. Majority of them are articles and prepositions like **a, in, the**, etc.

These words can take up much space or time. The good news is that **nltk** comes with a list of stop words and in **16 different languages**. We can then use these for parsing paragraphs of text then identify and remove the stop words from them. The following example demonstrates how to do this:

```python
import nltk
from nltk.corpus import stopwords

nltk.download('stopwords')
mylist = stopwords.words('english')
paragraph = "We have created a long paragraph of
text. You may have important words like Deep
Learning and Apple.Words that are not important
may be removed."
postPa = [word for word in paragraph.split() if
word not in mylist]
print(postPa)
```

When you execute the code, it will return the following:

```
['We', 'created', 'long', 'paragraph', 'text.', 'You', 'may', 'important', 'word
s', 'like', 'Deep', 'Learning', 'Apple.Words', 'important', 'may', 'removed.']
```

We began by importing the necessary libraries, including

all **stopwords** from **nltk.corpus**. The corpus refers to a large dataset of texts.

We have then defined a variable named **mylist** that will be used for storing the list of all English stop words.

We need a sample text that we will use for demonstrating text wrangling, hence we have defined a paragraph with text and assigned this to the variable **paragraph.**

We have then created a new variable and given it the name **postPa**. This variable contains an array of all the words contained in **paragraph** split up but does not include the words in **mylist.**

The above output shows that the text was split into different words and the stop words have been removed. Only the words that are considered important are shown in the above output. The prepositions and articles have been done away with.

From the above examples, you can tell that text wrangling and cleansing is an important procedure in **NLP** as it will ensure that you have the right or best data to work with. **NLTK** makes it possible for you to run complex algorithms on your text by use of only a few lines of code. You are allowed to split your text in the way that you want and do away with the unnecessary parts, and even make a reduction to it so that it may suit your logical computation. What we have done above with NLTK are only basics, but you will be able to appreciate the power of this library as you continue reading this book.

3-Replacing and Correcting words

When we are working with text, we will normally come across the incorrect text. Such text needs to be corrected. In NLP, there are numerous through which we can do this. Let us discuss them.

Converting Text to Lowercase

Once you get your text, it may be necessary for you to convert it into lowercase. This is possible in Python. We only have to call the **lower() function** provided by Python on our text and it will convert it into lowercase.

The following example demonstrates this:

```
myString = "The 5 countries include China, United
States, Indonesia, India,and Brazil."
str = myString.lower()
print(str)
```

The code will return the following upon execution:

```
the 5 countries include china, united states, indonesia, india,and brazil.
```

We have created a string of text and assigned it to the variable **myString**. We have then created the variable **str** and assigned it to the output of the operation where the above string is converted to lowercase. The value of this string has then been printed on the console.

If you want to work with the text while in uppercase, you can call the **upper() function** on it as demonstrated below:

```
myString = "The 5 countries include China, United
States, Indonesia, India, and Brazil."
str = myString.upper()
print(str)
```

The code should return the following output upon execution:

```
THE 5 COUNTRIES INCLUDE CHINA, UNITED STATES, INDONESIA, INDIA,AND BRAZIL.
```

Removing Numbers

In some cases, you may not want to work with numbers in your analysis. This means that they should be removed from the text. This can be done in Python using regular expressions. Consider the example given below:

```
import re
myString = 'Box A has 4 red and 6 white balls,
while Box B has 3 red and 5 blue balls.'
output = re.sub(r'\d+', '', myString)
print(output)
```

We have begun by importing the **re** library. This is the library that allows us to work with regular expressions in Python.

We have then defined a variable named **myString** and assigned it to a string with combined words and numbers. We have then called the **sub() method** provided by the re library to help us in substituting the integers. The **output** of this operation has been assigned to the variable named **output**. We have then printed the value of this variable on the console. The code will give the following result upon execution:

```
Box A has  red and  white balls, while Box B has  red and  blue balls.
```

The above output shows that the numbers have been removed from the text. You can now work with your text without numbers.

Removing Punctuation

You may want to remove a number of symbols from your text for easy processing. Examples of such symbols include #, $, %, *, & (), +, -, ., /, :, ;, <=>, ?, @, [\ ], ^, _ `, {, |, }, ~,]. Python provides us with a way of doing this.

The following code demonstrates this:

```
import string
myString = "This &is [a] string? {with} many.
punctuation.? marks!!!!"
output =
myString.translate(string.maketrans("",""),
string.punctuation)
print(output)
```

The code will remove all the punctuation marks from the string.

Removing Whitespace

You may want to work with text without leading and ending spaces. You can do away with these from your text by calling the **strip() method**. Here is an example:

```
myString = " \t a sample string\t "
str = myString.strip()
print(str)
```

We have defined a string and assigned it to the variable **myString**. this string has some whitespaces created by the **\t option (tab)**. We have then invoked the **strip() function** on the string and assigned the output to the variable str. We have then printed the value of this variable to the console. The code gives the following result:

```
a sample string
```

Part of Speech Tagging (POS)

The goal of POS is to assign the various parts of a speech to every word of the provided text like nouns, adjectives, verbs, etc. This is normally done based on the definition and the context.

There are various tools that provide us with POS taggers, including **NLTK, TextBlob,** etc. In this case, we will use **TextBlob** to demonstrate this. To install this library, run the following command on the terminal of your operating system:

```
pip3 install textblob
```

This should install the library. It should run quickly because you have already installed **NLTK.** After that, run the following code that demonstrates how speech tagging can be done:

```
from textblob import TextBlob
import nltk
nltk.download('averaged_perceptron_tagger')
myString = "Parts of speech: an article, to run,
fascinating, quickly, and, of"
output = TextBlob(myString)
print(output.tags)
```

The code should return the following output:

```
[('Parts', 'NNS'), ('of', 'IN'), ('speech', 'NN'), ('an', 'DT'), ('article', 'NN
'), ('to', 'TO'), ('run', 'VB'), ('fascinating', 'VBG'), ('quickly', 'RB'), ('an
d', 'CC'), ('of', 'IN')]
```

As you have noticed, each word in the text has been assigned to its right tag. This is because we invoked the **TextBlob() function** and passed the name of our string to it.

The output was then printed on the console.

Named entity Recognition

The purpose of named entity recognition in **NLP** is to identify the named entities in a set of text and assign them into the predefined categories such as locations, organizations, names of individuals, etc.

Let us demonstrate how this can be done using the **nltk** package:

```python
import nltk
from nltk import word_tokenize, pos_tag, ne_chunk
nltk.download('maxent_ne_chunker')
nltk.download('words')
myString = "He worked for Microsoft and attended a conference in Italy"
print(ne_chunk(pos_tag(word_tokenize(myString))))
```

The code should give the result given below upon execution:

```
(S
  He/PRP
  worked/VBD
  for/IN
  (ORGANIZATION Microsoft/NNP)
  and/CC
  attended/VBD
  a/DT
  conference/NN
  in/IN
  (GPE Italy/NNP))
```

We began by importing the **nltk** library and a number of functions from the same library. The necessary packages needed for named entity recognition, in this case, have been downloaded. We have then created a variable named **myString** and assigned a string to it. The functions have then been invoked on the string. The code will return the result given below upon execution:

```
(S
  He/PRP
  worked/VBD
  for/IN
  (ORGANIZATION Microsoft/NNP)
  and/CC
  attended/VBD
  a/DT
  conference/NN
  in/IN
  (GPE Italy/NNP))
```

Collocation Extraction

Collocations refer to words that occur together more frequently that it would happen by chance. Examples of collocations include **"free time"**, **"break the rules"**, **"by the way"**, **"keep in mind"**, **"get ready"** and many others. The following code demonstrates how these can be identified using **ICE**.

To install this module, run the following command:

```
pip3 install ICE
```

The command should install the package successfully. Now run the following command:

```
import ICE import CollocationExtractor
input=["she and Charlse duel with all keys on the line."]
```

```
extractor =
CollocationExtractor.with_collocation_pipeline("T
1" , bing_key = "Temp",pos_check = False)
print(extractor.get_collocations_of_length(input,
length = 3))
```

Finding Synonyms

We will use **wordnet**, which is an NLTK corpus reader, an English lexical database. We can use it to determine the meaning of a word, antonym or synonym. It can be defined as a semantically oriented English dictionary.

To import it from **nltk** corpus into our work space, we run the following command:

```
from nltk.corpus import wordnet
```

Synset is one of the features provided by wordnet. It is simply a collection of synonyms. Consider the example given below:

```
from nltk.corpus import wordnet
syn = wordnet.synsets("cat")
print(syn)
```

The code gives the following result upon execution:

```
[Synset('cat.n.01'), Synset('guy.n.01'), Synset('cat.n.03'), Synset('kat.n.01'),
Synset('cat-o'-nine-tails.n.01'), Synset('caterpillar.n.02'), Synset('big_cat.n
.01'), Synset('computerized_tomography.n.01'), Synset('cat.v.01'), Synset('vomit
.v.01')]
```

In the above example, we have invoked the **synsets() function** to give us the synonyms for the word cat. We have assigned the output to the variable named **syn**. We have then printed out the values of this variable on the console.

Wordnet also has a feature known as lexical relations which is a set of reciprocated semantic relations. Let us create a program that helps us to find the synonym and antonym of a certain word:

```python
from nltk.corpus import wordnet
synonyms = []
antonyms = []

for s in wordnet.synsets("passive"):
    for lemm in s.lemmas():
        synonyms.append(lemm.name())
        if lemm.antonyms():

antonyms.append(lemm.antonyms()[0].name())

            print(set(synonyms))
            print(set(antonyms))
```

In the above example, we are looking for **antonyms** and **synonyms** for the word **passive.**

We began by importing **wordnet** from **nltk.corpus.** We have then taken the list of antonyms and synonyms as empty and we will use these for appending purposes.

We have then passed the word **passive** to find its synonyms from the synsets module then we append them to the list synonyms and repeated it for the second one.

Finally, we have printed the output.

The code gives the result given below upon execution:

```
{'passive_voice'}
{'active_voice'}
{'passive_voice', 'passive'}
{'active_voice', 'active'}
{'passive_voice', 'passive', 'inactive', 'peaceful'}
{'active_voice', 'active'}
```

Fixing Word Lengthening

Word lengthening refers to the process of repeating characters. In English, words can only have a maximum of two characters repeated. Any additional characters should be done away with; otherwise, we may be dealing with misleading information. We can use the regular expressions' library to help us remove any repeated characters from our text. Let us create a function for doing that:

```python
import re
def remove_lengthening(text):
    patt = re.compile(r"(.)\1{2,}")
    return patt.sub(r"\1\1", text)

print(remove_lengthening( "commmmmmmmitttteeee" ))
```

The code will return the result given below when executed:

```
committee
```

We have created a function named **remove_lengthening** which takes our text as the input. We have then created a variable named **patt** which helps us define the pattern that characters in our words should take. We had three characters which had been lengthened, that is, **m, t** and **e**. The function has reduced them to two which is a perfect match. However, consider the following example:

```python
import re
def remove_lengthening(text):
    patt = re.compile(r"(.)\1{2,}")
    return patt.sub(r"\1\1", text)

print(remove_lengthening( "accccctive" ))
```

The code gives the following example upon execution:

```
acctive
```

The character c was lengthened. However, it was reduced to a length of **2**. The word is spelled as **"active"** rather than **"active"**. This shows why we need to do spelling correction even after reducing the lengthening.

Spell Correction

This is the process by which the spelling of a word is corrected. Spell correction algorithms work based on min-edit functions since brute forcing one's may take too much time.

For the mid-edit functions to work effectively, word lengthening should be used first. This means that our spell correction will depend on the word lengthening. NLTK comes with no spell correction module, but there are numerous other libraries that we can use to perform this task. We will be using pattern en for this task.

To install the library, run the following command:

```
pip3 install pattern
```

You can then write the following code to demonstrate how length removal and soell correction can be done in **NLP**:

```python
import re
from pattern.en import spelling

def remove_lengthening(text):
    patt = re.compile(r"(.)\1{2,}")
    return patt.sub(r"\1\1", text)

word = "acccccctiiiive"
word_wlf = remove_lengthening(word) #calling the
above function
print(word_wlf) #word lengthening cannot fix it
completely

final_word = spelling(word_wlf)
print(final_word)
```

We began by removing the lengthening. This was done by defining a function named **remove_lengthening**. It is in this method that we have defined that a word should not have a character that exceeds a length of **2**. When we passed the word acccccctiiiive to the function, it returned **acctiive**. However, the word is still not correct. We need to perform spell correction on the word. That is why we have invoked the **spelling()** **function** which we imported from **pattern.en** and passed the result of lengthening removal to it. This should return the correct spelling of the word which is **active**.

4-Text classification

There are numerous reasons as to why we may need to perform text classification. We may need to classify text as either education or politics or even military. We may be in need of classifying the text depending on the author who wrote it or based on gender. A great application of text classification is when you need to classify text as either spam or not spam, such as how email filters work. In this case, we will be creating a sentiment analysis algorithm.

The NLTK corpus comes with the movie reviews database, hence we will use it in this section. We will be using the words as the features and these are part of either a positive or negative movie review. This means that we can use this data for both training and testing.

Consider the following code:

```
import nltk
import random
from nltk.corpus import movie_reviews

nltk.download('movie_reviews')
docs = [(list(movie_reviews.words(fileid)),
category)
            for category in
movie_reviews.categories()
            for fileid in
movie_reviews.fileids(category)]

random.shuffle(docs)

print(docs[1])

all = []
for w in movie_reviews.words():
    all.append(w.lower())

all = nltk.FreqDist(all)
print(all.most_common(15))
print(all["entertainment"])
```

The movies' dataset is large, hence, it may take some time before it completes running.

Note that we started by downloading the dataset. Consider the following extracted from the above code:

```
docs = [(list(movie_reviews.words(fileid)),
category)
            for category in
movie_reviews.categories()
            for fileid in
movie_reviews.fileids(category)]
```

The above section of the code can be translated to: In every category (we have either pos or neg), take the entire file IDs (every review has own ID), then store the **word_tokenized** version (list of words) for the file ID, and then followed by the positive or negative label in one big list.

We have then used random to shuffle the documents. The reason is that we will do both training and testing. If we leave these in order, there are high chances that training will be done on all the negatives, a number of positives then testing will be done only against the positives. This is not we need to do; hence the data has been shuffled.

To be able to see the data that we are working with, we have printed out **docs [1]**, which is a big list with the first element being a list of words and the **2nd** element being the **"pos"** or **"neg"** label.

Our next intention is to collect all the words that we find; hence we may have a big list of typical words. It is from here that a frequency distribution can be performed to determine the most common words. Our goal is to store a few thousand words that are popular, hence this not be a problem for us.

The code returns the following output:

```
(['reading', 'the', 'cast', 'and', 'director',
'for', 'the', 'new', 'mobster', 'comedy', ',',
'"', 'analyze', 'this', ',', '"', 'i', 'asked',
'myself', ',', '"', 'how', 'could', 'this',
'miss', '?', '"', 'robert', 'de', 'niro', '(',
'"', 'taxi', 'driver', ',', '"', '"', 'raging',
'bull', '"', ')', ',', 'billy', 'crystal', '(',
'"', 'city', 'slickers', '"', ')', ',', 'lisa',
'kudrow', '(', '"', 'the', 'opposite', 'of',
'sex', '"', ')', ',', 'and', 'director',
'harold', 'ramis', '(', '"', 'national',
'lampoon', '"', 's', 'vacation', '"', ')', '.',
'these', 'are', 'usually', 'reliable',
'filmmakers', '(', 'well', ',', 'okay', ',',
'crystal', 'has', 'been', 'in', 'a', 'sizable',
```

'slump', 'lately', ')', ',', 'and', 'tellingly',
',', 'the', 'first', 'half', '-', 'hour', 'of',
'"', 'analyze', 'this', '"', 'was', 'very',
'funny', '.', 'unfortunately', ',', 'as', 'the',
'running', 'time', 'ticked', 'away', ',', 'i',
'began', 'to', 'think', 'that', 'the', 'first',
'thirty', 'minutes', 'had', ',', 'unbeknownst',
'to', 'me', ',', 'been', 'rewound', 'and',
'were', 'being', 'replayed', 'another', 'two', '-
', 'and', '-', 'a', '-', 'half', 'times', '.',
'the', 'film', 'has', 'obtained', 'a', 'clever',
'premise', ',', 'but', 'does', 'not', 'have',
'any', 'idea', 'what', 'to', 'do', 'with', 'it',
'as', 'it', 'progressively', 'becomes', 'more',
'and', 'more', 'repetitive', 'until', 'i',
'finally', 'stopped', 'enjoying', 'or', 'caring',
'about', 'what', 'was', 'happening', 'on', 'the',
'screen', '.', 'middle', '-', 'aged',
'psychoanalyst', 'ben', 'sobel', '"', 's', '(',
'billy', 'crystal', ')', 'life', 'is', 'finally',
'going', 'very', 'well', '.', 'although', 'he',
'has', 'never', 'gotten', 'along', 'with', 'his',
'own', 'uncaring', 'parents', ',', 'especially',
'his', 'father', ',', 'who', 'is', 'also', 'a',
'psychiatrist', ',', 'ben', 'has', 'an', 'easy',
'-', 'going', 'teenage', 'son', '(', 'kyle',
'sabihy', ')', 'and', 'is', 'about', 'to',
'travel', 'down', 'to', 'miami', 'to', 'get',
'married', 'to', 'his', 'tv', 'news', 'reporter',
'girlfriend', ',', 'laura', '(', 'lisa',
'kudrow', ')', '.', 'in', 'little', 'but', 'a',
'flash', ',', 'however', ',', 'ben', 'suddenly',
'sees', 'his', 'plans', 'ruined', 'when', 'he',
'accidentally', 'hits', 'the', 'car', 'of',
'the', 'mob', 'and', 'subsequently', 'gets',
'paid', 'a', 'visit', 'from', 'famed', 'mafia',
'guy', 'paul', 'vitti', '(', 'robert', 'de',
'niro', ')', ',', 'who', 'desperately', 'wants',
'counseling', ',', 'even', 'though', 'he',
'himself', 'won', '"', 't', 'even', 'admit',
'to', 'having', 'anxiety', 'attacks', '.', 'ben',
'tries', 'to', 'help', 'paul', ',', 'mostly',
'so', 'he', 'will', 'get', 'him', 'off', 'his',
'back', ',', 'but', 'the', 'plot', 'gets',

'more', 'complicated', 'when', 'paul', 'follows',
'ben', 'to', 'his', 'wedding', ',', 'which',
'ends', 'with', 'a', 'man', 'dropping', 'eight',
'stories', 'to', 'his', 'death', '.', 'it',
'seems', 'to', 'ben', 'that', 'no', 'matter',
'what', 'he', 'does', ',', 'paul', 'vitti',
'will', 'not', 'go', 'away', ',', 'and', 'the',
'more', 'they', 'become', 'involved', ',', 'the',
'more', 'ben', "'", 's', 'potentially', 'happy',
'life', 'gets', 'into', 'danger', '.', '"',
'analyze', 'this', '"', 'has', 'a', 'few',
'laughs', 'sprinkled', 'throughout', '(',
'mostly', 'in', 'the', 'first', 'half', ')', ',',
'but', 'i', 'always', 'had', 'the', 'nagging',
'thought', 'that', 'what', 'director', 'ramis',
'and', 'writers', 'peter', 'tolan', ',', 'ramis',
',', 'and', 'kenneth', 'lonergan', 'had', 'done',
'was', 'thought', 'of', 'one', 'joke', '(',
'robert', 'de', 'niro', 'lightly', 'spoofing',
'his', 'serious', 'past', 'mafia', 'roles', ',',
'while', 'terrorizing', 'and', 'becoming',
'buddies', 'with', 'comic', 'billy', 'crystal',
')', 'and', 'then', 'tiresomely', 'recycled',
'it', 'for', 'the', 'duration', 'of', 'the',
'106', '-', 'minute', 'running', 'time', '.',
'admittedly', ',', 'de', 'niro', 'is', 'very',
'funny', 'here', '(', 'and', 'i', 'can', "'",
't', 'remember', 'the', 'last', 'time', 'you',
'could', 'use', 'that', 'adjective', 'to',
'describe', 'him', ')', ',', 'and', 'crystal',
'is', 'in', 'top', '-', 'form', ',', 'but',
'the', 'whole', 'movie', 'is', 'weighed', 'down',
'directly', 'on', 'their', 'shoulders', 'with',
'nothing', 'else', 'to', 'support', 'them', ',',
'including', 'a', 'substantial', 'plotline', '.',
'since', '"', 'analyze', 'this', '"', 'bills',
'not', 'one', ',', 'not', 'two', ',', 'but',
'three', 'writers', ',', 'you', "'", 'd',
'think', 'that', 'they', 'would', 'have', 'been',
'able', 'to', 'work', 'together', 'to', 'fix',
'the', 'noticably', 'large', 'flaws', ',', 'but',
'they', 'must', 'have', 'all', 'been', 'on',
'auto', '-', 'pilot', '.', 'one', 'of', 'the',

'most', 'disappointing', 'and', 'wasted',
'opportunities', 'in', 'the', 'film', 'is',
'the', 'way', 'the', 'movie', 'deals', 'with',
'the', 'supporting', 'characters', ',', 'all',
'of', 'which', 'have', 'next', 'to', 'nothing',
'to', 'do', 'and', 'aren', "'", 't', 'even',
'given', 'multi', '-', 'dimensional',
'characters', 'to', 'attempt', 'to', 'develop',
'.', 'coming', 'off', 'of', 'her', 'oscar', '-',
'caliber', 'work', 'in', 'two', 'of', 'last',
'year', "'", 's', 'best', 'films', ',', '"',
'clockwatchers', '"', 'and', '"', 'the',
'opposite', 'of', 'sex', ',', '"', 'lisa',
'kudrow', "'", 's', 'throwaway', '"',
'girlfriend', '"', 'role', 'is', 'an',
'incredible', 'step', 'down', '.', 'sure', ',',
'kudrow', "'", 's', 'fellow', '"', 'friend', '"',
'jennifer', 'aniston', 'did', 'the', 'same',
'thing', 'two', 'weeks', 'ago', 'in', '"',
'office', 'space', ',', '"', 'but', 'at',
'least', 'we', 'got', 'to', 'spend', 'a',
'little', 'time', 'with', 'aniston', '.',
'kudrow', ',', 'meanwhile', ',', 'mostly',
'just', 'stands', 'around', ',', 'no', 'doubt',
'wondering', 'why', 'she', 'agreed', 'to',
'appear', 'in', 'this', 'film', 'in', 'the',
'first', 'place', '.', 'chazz', 'palminteri',
',', 'as', 'rival', 'gangster', 'primo', ',',
'fares', 'even', 'worse', ',', 'in', 'a', 'role',
'that', 'plays', 'more', 'like', 'an',
'afterthought', 'than', 'an', 'actual',
'character', '.', 'finally', ',', 'molly',
'shannon', '(', 'rising', 'film', 'star', 'and',
'cast', 'member', 'on', '"', 'saturday', 'night',
'live', '"', ')', 'has', 'a', 'rousingly',
'hilarious', 'one', '-', 'scene', 'cameo',
'right', 'at', 'the', 'beginning', 'as', 'one',
'of', 'crystal', "'", 's', 'patients', 'and',
'then', 'completely', 'disappears', '.', 'too',
'bad', ',', 'considering', 'that', 'the',
'supporting', 'actors', 'surely', 'have',
'proven', 'that', 'they', 'have', 'the',
'abilities', 'to', 'support', 'de', 'niro',
'and', 'crystal', '.', 'once', '"', 'analyze',

'this', '"', 'approached', 'its', 'second',
'wedding', 'scene', 'leaving', 'kudrow', "'",
's', 'laura', 'standing', 'alone', 'at', 'the',
'altar', 'once', 'again', ',', 'i', 'had',
'become', 'thoroughly', 'annoyed', 'by', 'where',
'the', 'story', 'had', 'gone', ',', 'and', 'had',
'mostly', 'lost', 'respect', 'for', 'the',
'character', 'we', 'were', 'supposed', 'to',
'sympathize', 'with', 'the', 'most', ',', 'ben',
'.', 'afterwards', ',', 'the', 'climactic',
'scene', 'with', 'ben', 'posing', 'as', 'a',
'fellow', 'mob', 'boss', 'in', 'place', 'of',
'the', 'depressed', 'paul', ',', 'became', 'a',
'real', 'laugh', '-', 'free', 'dead', '-',
'zone', ',', 'losing', 'its', 'last',
'remaining', 'comic', 'punches', '.', '"',
'analyze', 'this', '"', 'proves', 'that',
'talent', 'can', 'certainly', 'help', 'any',
'film', 'out', ',', 'but', 'when', 'the',
'written', 'material', 'isn', '"', 't', 'up',
'to', 'their', 'level', ',', 'what', 'we', 'are',
'virtually', 'left', 'with', 'is', 'a', 'vacuum',
'of', 'thin', 'air', '.'], 'neg')
[(',', 77717), ('the', 76529), ('.', 65876),
('a', 38106), ('and', 35576), ('of', 34123),
('to', 31937), ("'", 30585), ('is', 25195),
('in', 21822), ('s', 18513), ('"', 17612), ('it',
16107), ('that', 15924), ('-', 15595)]
211

The **211** shown above tells us the word **entertainment** occurs 211 times.

To know the **10** most common words, we can run the following command:

```
print(all.most_common(10))
```

This returns the following:

```
>>> print(all.most_common(10))
[(',', 77717), ('the', 76529), ('.', 65876), ('a', 38106), ('and', 35576), ('of'
, 34123), ('to', 31937), ('"'", 30585), ('is', 25195), ('in', 21822)]
>>>
```

Converting Text to Features

In this section, we will be compiling feature lists of the words from the positive reviews and words from negative reviews to be able to see trends in the specific types of words in positive or negative reviews. Modify your previous code to the following:

```python
import nltk
import random
from nltk.corpus import movie_reviews

nltk.download('movie_reviews')
docs = [(list(movie_reviews.words(fileid)),
category)
            for category in
movie_reviews.categories()
            for fileid in
movie_reviews.fileids(category)]

random.shuffle(docs)

print(docs[1])

all = []
for w in movie_reviews.words():
    all.append(w.lower())

all = nltk.FreqDist(all)
word_features = list(all.keys())[:3000]
```

Notice that we have introduced a new variable with the name **word_features**. This variable will hold the most popular

3000 words. We now need to create a function that will help us find these words from both the positive and negative documents, with their presence being marked as either positive or negative. Here is the function:

```
def search_features(doc):
    words = set(doc)
    features = {}
    for w in word_features:
        features[w] = (w in words)

    return features
```

Note that the function has been given the name **search_features**.

We can now go ahead and print one feature set:

```
print(search_features(movie_reviews.words('neg/cv
000_29416.txt')))
```

You should now have the following code:

```
import nltk
import random
from nltk.corpus import movie_reviews

nltk.download('movie_reviews')
docs = [(list(movie_reviews.words(fileid)),
category)
            for category in
movie_reviews.categories()
            for fileid in
movie_reviews.fileids(category)]

random.shuffle(docs)

print(docs[1])
```

```
all = []
for w in movie_reviews.words():
    all.append(w.lower())

all = nltk.FreqDist(all)
word_features = list(all.keys())[:3000]


def search_features(doc):
    words = set(doc)
    features = {}
    for w in word_features:
        features[w] = (w in words)

    return features

print(search_features(movie_reviews.words('neg/cv
000_29416.txt')))
```

Here is a section of the output that you should get upon executing the above code:

```
False, 'rustler': False, 'edifice': False,
'mystify': False, 'oracle': False, 'sirocco':
False, 'combatants': False, 'osemt': False,
'acclaim': False, 'dunsworth': False,
'unexpectantly': False, 'starving': False,
'freedman': False, 'accursed': False, 'jams':
False, 'greys': False, 'wrecked': False,
'projecting': False, 'geraldo': False,
'prominent': False, 'stacy': False, 'generic':
False, 'unperturbed': False, 'polish': False,
'gosse': False, 'chrysler': False, 'loyal':
False, 'hither': False, 'aried': False,
'coarser': False, 'newfoundland': False,
'gradisca': False, 'danish': False, 'mckee':
False, 'keyser': False, 'unveil': False,
'gisbourne': False, 'telegraphing': False,
'prescott': False, 'lighweight': False,
'balancing': False, 'balsan': False,
'incorporating': False, 'ulysses': False,
```

'title': **False**, 'zestful': **False**, 'camel': **False**,
'iraq': **False**, 'handiwork': **False**, 'friendly':
False, 'carvey': **False**, 'enzyme': **False**,
'lynching': **False**, 'railed': **False**, 'croaker':
False, 'unlocks': **False**, 'replenishing': **False**,
'dubey': **False**, 'tram': **False**, 'signy': **False**,
'firmest': **False**, '37th': **False**, 'confronts':
False, 'gutting': **False**, 'poisoned': **False**,
'shocks': **False**, 'condemning': **False**, 'outward':
False, 'semester': **False**, 'whitechapel': **False**,
'dispels': **False**, 'hurl': **False**, 'barkin': **False**,
'declared': **False**, 'upheaval': **False**, 'catania':
False, 'arcane': **False**, 'coughlan': **False**,
'morse': **False**, 'invoking': **False**, 'rebuilding':
False, 'cleave': **False**, 'publishers': **False**,
'onw': **False**, 'coaxed': **False**, 'laertes': **False**,
'engross': **False**, 'studebakers': **False**,
'darling': **False**, 'isuro': **False**, 'banquets':
False, 'mathieu': **False**, 'insisting': **False**,
'madio': **False**, 'seminal': **False**, 'mimic': **False**,
'expirating': **False**, 'reinterpretation': **False**,
'rejections': **False**, 'aaaaaaaaah': **False**,
'digressions': **False**, 'detestable': **False**,
'torching': **False**, 'regulation': **False**,
'infuriates': **False**, 'adherents': **False**,
'contested': **False**, 'stripping': **False**, 'permit':
False, 'schumaccer': **False**, 'lfe': **False**,
'fortinbras': **False**, 'shoestring': **False**,
'henceforth': **False**, 'telekinetically': **False**,
'yippee': **False**, 'homies': **False**, 'vadis': **False**,
'ye': **False**, 'instructors': **False**, 'nikki':
False, 'bots': **False**, 'monologues': **False**,
'hypocrisy': **False**, '10th': **False**, 'unnatural':
False, 'mathou': **False**, 'refugee': **False**, 'moff':
False, 'arranging': **False**, 'iris': **False**,
'portorican': **False**, 'changwei': **False**, '2002':
False, 'irresistable': **False**, 'katt': **False**,
'panthers': **False**, 'concerto': **False**,
'obssessively': **False**, 'astaire': **False**, 'abbe':
False, 'tranisition': **False**, 'hypnotherapist':
False, 'tearfully': **False**, 'stinker': **False**,
'heartwrenching': **False**, 'diesel': **False**,
'whines': **False**, 'capably': **False**, 'hum': **False**,

```
'foreknowledge': False, 'hauff': False, '48th':
False, 'sloppiness': False, 'cyrus': False,
'agonisingly': False, 'recognizably': False,
'masaya': False, 'briefly': False,
'incompetency': False, 'burgeoning': False,
'exclaim': False, 'cinematogrophy': False,
'victorious': False, 'skirts': False, 'visage':
False, 'sillas': False, 'preachings': False,
'gast': False, 'doves': False, 'bezucha': False,
'herded': False, 'transistion': False,
'lansquenet': False, 'consumerism': False,
'brick': False, 'included': False, 'blatancy':
False, 'brable': False}
```

We can then do it for all the documents as we save the feature existence **Booleans** together with their respective positive or negative categories. We can do that as follows:

```
featuresets = [(search_features(rev), category)
for (rev, category) in docs]
```

At this point, we have both the features and the labels. We can now train our algorithm and test it.

Naïve Bayes Classifier

We now need to choose the algorithm to use then divide our data into training and test sets. We will use Naive Bayes as the algorithm. It is a very popular algorithm when it comes to solving classification problems. Before we can train and test our algorithm, we should first split our data into training and test sets.

We could have used the same dataset for training and testing but this will lead to serious bias issues, hence training and testing should never be done using the same dataset. Since our dataset has been shuffled, the first **1,900** shuffled reviews shall be assigned, and these will consist of both the positive and the negative reviews as the training set. The remaining **100** can then be used to perform the test and see how accurate we are.

Since our data is labeled, this process is referred to as **supervised learning**. The reason is that we are telling the algorithm that certain data is positive or certain data is negative. Once the training has been done, the machine will be shown some new data and asked to classify it based on what it learned from the training. Let us now split the data:

```
# define the dataset to be used for training the
classifier
training_set = featuresets[:1900]

# define the dataset to be used for testing the
classifier
testing_set = featuresets[1900:]
```

We can then define and train the classifier as shown below:

```
classifier =
nltk.NaiveBayesClassifier.train(training_set)
```

In the above line, we have simply invoked the naive bayes classifier, then we have called the **train** method on the classifier, all this in one line. Notice that the name of our training data set has been passed to the function.

The classifier has been trained, hence we can now go ahead and test it. This can be done as follows:

```
classifier =
```

```
nltk.NaiveBayesClassifierprint("Classifier
accuracy
percentage:",(nltk.classify.accuracy(classifier,
testing_set))*100)
```

Note that we testing while at the same time we have the correct answers. So, the computer is given the data without the answers so that we can tell whether it guesses or gets the answers right. Since the data has been shuffled, we will end up getting up a varying accuracy.

We can now get to know the most valuable words when it comes to either positive or negative reviews. This can be done as follows:

```
classifier.show_most_informative_features(10).tra
in(training_set)
```

At this point, you should have the following code:

```
import nltk
import random
from nltk.corpus import movie_reviews

nltk.download('movie_reviews')
docs = [(list(movie_reviews.words(fileid)),
category)
            for category in
movie_reviews.categories()
            for fileid in
movie_reviews.fileids(category)]

random.shuffle(docs)

print(docs[1])

all = []
for w in movie_reviews.words():
    all.append(w.lower())
```

```python
all = nltk.FreqDist(all)
word_features = list(all.keys())[:3000]


def search_features(doc):
    words = set(doc)
    features = {}
    for w in word_features:
        features[w] = (w in words)

    return features


# define the dataset to be used for testing the classifier
testing_set = featuresets[1900:]

classifier = nltk.NaiveBayesClassifier.train(training_set)

print("Classifier accuracy percentage:",(nltk.classify.accuracy(classifier, testing_set))*100)
classifier.show_most_informative_features(10)
```

Here is a section of output from the code:

```
tforward', ',', 'so', 'quaint', ',', 'that',
'it', 'ultimately', 'becomes', 'charming', '.',
'though', 'i', 'enjoy', 'the', 'complex',
'plotting', 'of', 'film', 'noir', 'as', 'much',
'as', 'the', 'next', 'person', ',', 'when', 'it',
'comes', 'to', 'family', 'entertainment', ',',
'simple', 'is', 'the', 'way', 'to', 'go', '.',
'it', "'", 's', 'akin', 'to', 'one', 'of',
'those', 'bedtime', 'stories', 'your', 'father',
'told', 'that', 'had', 'you', 'hanging', 'on',
'his', 'every', 'word', ',', 'but', 'it', "'",
's', 'not', 'the', 'story', 'that', 'sets',
'the', 'film', 'above', 'others', 'of', 'its',
'kind', ',', 'but', 'rather', 'the', 'elements',
'that', 'go', 'into', 'the', 'story', ',',
'namely', 'real', 'characters', 'and',
```

```
'thoughtful', 'dialogue', ',', 'which', '"',
'the', 'iron', 'giant', '"', 'has', 'in',
'spades', '.'], 'pos')
Classifier accuracy percentage: 73.0
Most Informative Features
                    deft = True                  pos
  : neg      =        8.9 : 1.0
                thematic = True                  pos
  : neg      =        8.9 : 1.0
                 layered = True                  pos
  : neg      =        7.6 : 1.0
                 detract = True                  pos
  : neg      =        7.6 : 1.0
                  turkey = True                  neg
  : pos      =        6.7 : 1.0
                   anger = True                  pos
  : neg      =        6.0 : 1.0
                  justin = True                  neg
  : pos      =        5.9 : 1.0
                  guinea = True                  neg
  : pos      =        5.8 : 1.0
                  mating = True                  neg
  : pos      =        5.8 : 1.0
               biologist = True                  neg
  : pos      =        5.8 : 1.0
```

The above output shows that the classifier gave us an accuracy of **73.0** percent. This is a good percentage. We also have the list of the top 10 most important words in terms of giving us information. This gives us the ratio of occurrences in negative to positive, or the vice versa, for each word. From the above output, you can tell that the word **mating** appears **5.8** more times in the negative reviews than in the positive reviews. And the word **justin 5.9** more times.

Our classifier now seems to be reliable and we can use it to predict the results of new data. It will not be practical for us to be training the classifier any time we need to use it for this. To avoid this, you can save your classifier by use of the pickle module.

Saving the Classifier

Training classifiers takes a long time. Imagine you have to train the classifier every time that you want to use it, especially when a large dataset is involved. This will cost you much time and effort. However, you can use the pickle module to serialize a classifier object so that you only have to load it every time you need to use it.

To do this, your first step should be saving the object. This means that you should first import the pickle module at the top of your script. Once you have called the **.train() classifier** for training, you can invoke the lines given below to save it:

```
save_classifier = open("naivebayes.pickle","wb")
pickle.dump(classifier, save_classifier)
save_classifier.close()
```

The code will open a **pickle file** while preparing to write some data in bytes. To dump the data, we can call **pickle.dump().** However, this needs that you pass parameters to it. The first parameter should be what you need to dump, and the second parameter is where you need to dump it. After that, you can close the file you will have serialized or saved it.

Now that we have saved the classifier, how can we access it and use it? The .pickle file that we created is a serialized object. Our task at this point is to read it into the computer memory, and this process should be quick just like the way you read other files. The following code demonstrates how you can do this:

```
classifier_f = open("naivebayes.pickle", "rb")
classifier = pickle.load(classifier_f)
classifier_f.close()
```

We have opened the file to be read as bytes. We have then loaded the file by calling **pickle.load()** and the data has been saved in a variable named **classifier**. The file has then been closed. We have our classifier object!

It is now possible for us to use the object without having to train the classifier every time that we need to use it.

5-Sentiment Analysis

Sentiment analysis is also known as **Opinion analysis**. It is a branch of natural language processing that deals with identifying and extracting opinion from a text. The goal of sentiment analysis is to gauge the sentiments, attitudes, evaluations, and emotions of a writer or speaker depending on the computational treatment of the subjectivity in the text.

Today, most businesses rely on data. However, most of this data is unstructured as it comes from sources like chats, emails, social media, articles, surveys and documents. The user content obtained from Twitter and Facebook comes with a lot of challenges, not only because of the amount of data but because of the kind of language used by some users, that is, emoticons, memes, short form, etc.

It can be tough to sift through this data, taking us a much longer time. Also, much expertise and resources are needed for this. This means that it's not easy to analyze such data.

Sentiment analysis has proved to be important for researchers and practitioners, especially those in the fields of marketing, sociology, psychology, advertising, political science and economics as all of these rely on human-computer interaction data.

With sentiment analysis, companies are able to make sense out of data since the process of analyzing data is automated. This means that they are able to extract useful insights from vast amounts of unstructured without having to do so manually.

VADER Sentiment Analysis

VADER stands for **Valence Aware Dictionary** and **sentiment Reasoner**. It is a rule-based and lexicon sentiment analysis tool used to analyze social media sentiments. It comes with a list of lexical features that are labeled according to their semantic orientation which is either negative or positive.

VADER has proved to be very good for analyzing social media **texts**, **movie reviews**, **NY Times editorials**, and **product reviews**. The reason behind this is that VADER does not only tell us about the negative or positive score but it also tells about how positive or negative the score is.

VADER is open source and under the MIT license. To use it, you have to install it. This can be done easily by use of the pip package as shown below:

```
pip3 install vaderSentiment
```

Once it has been installed, you can Import it and create its object so that you can work with it. The following code demonstrates how you can do this:

```
from vaderSentiment.vaderSentiment import
SentimentIntensityAnalyzer
analyser = SentimentIntensityAnalyzer()
```

In the above code, we have imported the **SentimentIntensityAnalyzer** **functiom** **vaderSentiment.vaderSentiment**. We have then created an instance of this function and given it the name **analyser**.

Working and Scoring

We can now test the **VADER** on our first sentiment. We will use a method named **polarity_scores()** to get the polarity indices of a given sentence. Let us first create a function:

```
def sentiment_analyzer_scores(sentence):
    score = analyser.polarity_scores(sentence)
    print("{:-<40} {}".format(sentence,
str(score)))
```

We have created a function named **sentiment_analyzer_scores()** that takes in a sentence as the parameter. We have then invoked the **polarity_scores() method** and passed the parameter **sentence** to it. the invocation has been done via the object of the method that we created previously and the result has been assigned to the **score** variable.

Let us then pass a review and see how VADER will be able to analyze it:

```
print(sentiment_analyzer_scores("The car is
cool!"))
```

You should now have the following code:

```
from vaderSentiment.vaderSentiment import
SentimentIntensityAnalyzer
analyser = SentimentIntensityAnalyzer()

def sentiment_analyzer_scores(sentence):
    score = analyser.polarity_scores(sentence)
    print("{:-<40} {}".format(sentence,
str(score)))

print(sentiment_analyzer_scores("The car is
cool!"))
```

The code returns the following result upon execution:

```
The car is cool!----------------------- {'neu': 0.536, 'pos': 0.464, 'compound'
: 0.3802, 'neg': 0.0}
None
```

The above output shows that there is a positive, negative and neutral score for the text or review. Each of these scores shows the proportion of text that falls within these categories. All of these scores should add up to 1.

The compound score denotes a metric that calculates the sum of all lexicon ratings with normalization of between -1 (the most extreme negative) and +1 (the most extreme positive).

When analyzing comments, there are key points that VADER relies on. These include the following:

Punctuation

When an exclamation mark **(!)** is encountered, the magnitude of the intensity will be increased without modification to the semantic orientation. For example, **"The car is cool!"** is more intense compared to **"The car is cool."** Again, when you use many! The magnitude will also increase.

Let us demonstrate the above by using an example:

Here is the base sentence:

```python
from vaderSentiment.vaderSentiment import
SentimentIntensityAnalyzer
analyser = SentimentIntensityAnalyzer()

def sentiment_analyzer_scores(sentence):
    score = analyser.polarity_scores(sentence)
    print("{:-<40} {}".format(sentence,
str(score)))

print(sentiment_analyzer_scores("The car is
cool"))
```

```
>>> print(sentiment_analyzer_scores("The car is cool"))
The car is cool--------------------------- {'neu': 0.566, 'pos': 0.434, 'compound'
: 0.3182, 'neg': 0.0}
None
>>>
```

Let us check how the scores change when we change the punctuation:

```python
from vaderSentiment.vaderSentiment import
SentimentIntensityAnalyzer
analyser = SentimentIntensityAnalyzer()

def sentiment_analyzer_scores(sentence):
    score = analyser.polarity_scores(sentence)
```

```
    print("{:-<40} {}".format(sentence,
str(score)))

print(sentiment_analyzer_scores("The car is
cool!"))
```

```
>>> print(sentiment_analyzer_scores("The car is cool!"))
The car is cool!----------------------- {'neu': 0.536, 'pos': 0.464, 'compound'
: 0.3802, 'neg': 0.0}
None
>>>
```

```
from vaderSentiment.vaderSentiment import
SentimentIntensityAnalyzer
analyser = SentimentIntensityAnalyzer()

def sentiment_analyzer_scores(sentence):
    score = analyser.polarity_scores(sentence)
    print("{:-<40} {}".format(sentence,
str(score)))

print(sentiment_analyzer_scores("The car is
cool!!"))
```

```
>>> print(sentiment_analyzer_scores("The car is cool!!"))
The car is cool!!---------------------- {'neu': 0.51, 'pos': 0.49, 'compound':
0.4374, 'neg': 0.0}
None
>>>
```

```
from vaderSentiment.vaderSentiment import
SentimentIntensityAnalyzer
analyser = SentimentIntensityAnalyzer()

def sentiment_analyzer_scores(sentence):
    score = analyser.polarity_scores(sentence)
    print("{:-<40} {}".format(sentence,
str(score)))

print(sentiment_analyzer_scores("The car is
cool!!!"))
```

```
>>> print(sentiment_analyzer_scores("The car is cool!!!"))
The car is cool!!!--------------------- {'neu': 0.486, 'pos': 0.514, 'compound'
: 0.4898, 'neg': 0.0}
None
>>>
```

The overall compound score is increasing with every! that you add.

Capitalization

When you use an upper case letter to put emphasis on a sentiment-relevant word and make the other letters lowercase, this will increase the magnitude of the sentiment intensity. A good example is, *The car is COOL!* has a high magnitude on the sentiment intensity than *The car is cool!* Let us demonstrate this using an example:

```
from vaderSentiment.vaderSentiment import
SentimentIntensityAnalyzer
analyser = SentimentIntensityAnalyzer()

def sentiment_analyzer_scores(sentence):
    score = analyser.polarity_scores(sentence)
    print("{:-<40} {}".format(sentence,
str(score)))

print(sentiment_analyzer_scores("The car is
COOL!"))
```

```
>>> print(sentiment_analyzer_scores("The car is COOL!"))
The car is COOL!------------------------ {'neu': 0.474, 'pos': 0.526, 'compound'
: 0.5147, 'neg': 0.0}
None
>>>
```

```
from vaderSentiment.vaderSentiment import
SentimentIntensityAnalyzer
analyser = SentimentIntensityAnalyzer()

def sentiment_analyzer_scores(sentence):
    score = analyser.polarity_scores(sentence)
```

```
print("{:-<40} {}".format(sentence,
str(score)))

print(sentiment_analyzer_scores("The car is
cool!"))
```

```
>>> print(sentiment_analyzer_scores("The car is cool!"))
The car is cool!------------------------ {'neu': 0.536, 'pos': 0.464, 'compound'
: 0.3802, 'neg': 0.0}
None
>>>
```

Degree Modifiers

These are also known as intensifiers and they affect the intensity of the sentiment by either increasing or decreasing it. For example, *The car is extremely cool!* is more intense compared to, *The car is cool!*

```
from vaderSentiment.vaderSentiment import
SentimentIntensityAnalyzer
analyser = SentimentIntensityAnalyzer()

def sentiment_analyzer_scores(sentence):
    score = analyser.polarity_scores(sentence)
    print("{:-<40} {}".format(sentence,
str(score)))

print(sentiment_analyzer_scores("The car is
cool!"))
```

The code returns the following:

```
The car is cool!------------------------ {'neu': 0.536, 'neg': 0.0, 'compound':
0.3802, 'pos': 0.464}
None
```

```
from vaderSentiment.vaderSentiment import
SentimentIntensityAnalyzer
analyser = SentimentIntensityAnalyzer()
```

```
def sentiment_analyzer_scores(sentence):
    score = analyser.polarity_scores(sentence)
    print("{:-<40} {}".format(sentence,
str(score)))

print(sentiment_analyzer_scores("The car is
marginally cool!"))
```

The code returns the following:

```
The car is marginally cool!------------- {'pos': 0.365, 'compound': 0.318, 'neu'
: 0.635, 'neg': 0.0}
None
```

```
from vaderSentiment.vaderSentiment import
SentimentIntensityAnalyzer
analyser = SentimentIntensityAnalyzer()

def sentiment_analyzer_scores(sentence):
    score = analyser.polarity_scores(sentence)
    print("{:-<40} {}".format(sentence,
str(score)))

print(sentiment_analyzer_scores("The car is
extremely cool!"))
```

The code returns the following:

```
The car is extremely cool!-------------- {'neu': 0.581, 'compound': 0.4376, 'neg
': 0.0, 'pos': 0.419}
None
```

We have used the text first without a degree intensifier, then we have modified it to add two different degree intensifiers. In all cases, you must have noticed that the compound score increased when we added the degree modifiers.

Conjunctions

The use of a conjunction such as but shows a change in in the polarity of sentiment, and the sentiment of the text that follows the conjunction becomes dominant. For example, "I enjoyed your hotel food, but I didn't like the way waiters offer their services." The statement has a mixed sentiment, and the latter part dictates the overall rating. This is demonstrated in the following example:

```
from vaderSentiment.vaderSentiment import
SentimentIntensityAnalyzer
analyser = SentimentIntensityAnalyzer()

def sentiment_analyzer_scores(sentence):
    score = analyser.polarity_scores(sentence)
    print("{:-<40} {}".format(sentence,
str(score)))

print(sentiment_analyzer_scores("I enjoyed your
hotel food, but I didn't like the way waiters
offer their services"))
```

The code returns the following result:

```
I enjoyed your hotel food, but I didn't like the way waiters offer their service
s {'neu': 0.671, 'pos': 0.329, 'neg': 0.0, 'compound': 0.6597}
None
```

Preceding Tri-gram

When we examine the tri-gram that precedes sentiment-laden lexical feature, we get almost **90%** of all cases in which negation flips the polarity of text in question. An example of a negated sentence is, *"Your hotel services are not that great."*

```python
from vaderSentiment.vaderSentiment import
SentimentIntensityAnalyzer
analyser = SentimentIntensityAnalyzer()

def sentiment_analyzer_scores(sentence):
    score = analyser.polarity_scores(sentence)
    print("{:-<40} {}".format(sentence,
str(score)))

print(sentiment_analyzer_scores("Your hotel
services are not that great"))
```

The code returns the result given below:

```
Your hotel services are not that great-- {'neg': 0.354, 'compound': -0.5096, 'po
s': 0.0, 'neu': 0.646}
None
```

6-Parsing Structure in Text

Syntactic parsing refers to a technique by which tokenized, segmented and part-of-speech segmented text is assigned a structure revealing the relationship between tokens that are governed by syntax rules such as grammars.

Syntax parses are usually done as the first step in deep information extraction and semantic understanding of a text. However, note that syntax parsing methods usually suffer from **structural ambiguity**, which means that we could have more than one correct parse trees for one sentence. This may present a challenge to selecting the most likely parse for the sentence.

Currently, the best syntax parser that supports English, Arabic, French, German, Chinese, and Spanish languages are the blackbox that is found in **Stanford's CoreNLP Library**. It is a Java library and it requires to have installed **Java 1.8**. The good thing about this is that it also comes with a server that you can access from Python by use of the **nltk library**.

Chunking (Shallow Parsing)

Chunking refers to the process of identifying the constituent parts of a sentence such as a **verb, nouns, adjectives**, etc. These are then linked to the higher order units with discrete grammatical meanings such as **noun groups, verb groups**, etc. Let us demonstrate this using an example.

The purpose of chunking is to group text into groups that are more meaningful. These groups are known as **noun phrases**. The idea is to group the words in such a way that the related words are grouped together. The group of words that you create from chunking is known as **chunks**.

We should first determine the parts of speech of every word:

```
from textblob import TextBlob
myString = "John found a new coach and a new bed
in his new apartment."
output = TextBlob(myString)
print(output.tags)
```

This should return the following:

```
[('John', 'NNP'), ('found', 'VBD'), ('a', 'DT'), ('new', 'JJ'), ('coach', 'NN'),
('and', 'CC'), ('a', 'DT'), ('new', 'JJ'), ('bed', 'NN'), ('in', 'IN'), ('his',
'PRP$'), ('new', 'JJ'), ('apartment', 'NN')]
```

We imported the **TextBlob** function from the textblob package. We created a string named **myString** and invoked this function on the string. That is tagging has been done.

Now that we have done tagging, we can proceed to the next step which is chunking. The following code demonstrates how to do it:

```
reg_exp = "NP: {<DT>?<JJ>*<NN>}"
rp = nltk.RegexpParser(reg_exp)
output = rp.parse(output.tags)
print(output)
```

At this point, you should have the following code:

```
import nltk
from textblob import TextBlob
myString = "John found a new coach and a new bed in his new apartment."
output = TextBlob(myString)

reg_exp = "NP: {<DT>?<JJ>*<NN>}"
rp = nltk.RegexpParser(reg_exp)
output = rp.parse(output.tags)
print(output)
```

Upon execution, you should get the result given below:

```
(S
  John/NNP
  found/VBD
  (NP a/DT new/JJ coach/NN)
  and/CC
  (NP a/DT new/JJ bed/NN)
  in/IN
  his/PRP$
  (NP new/JJ apartment/NN))
```

We began by importing the **nltk package** and then the **TextBlob** function from the textblob library. We have then created a string and assigned it to the variable named **myString**. The **TextBlob function** has then been invoked on this string for tagging purpose. The variable **output** has been

defined and assigned the result of chunking or parsing. We
have then printed the result on the console.

It is possible for us to draw the tree structure of the
sentence. To achieve this, we just achieve the **draw() method**
on the output as shown below:

```
import nltk
from textblob import TextBlob
myString = "John found a new coach and a new bed
in his new apartment."
output = TextBlob(myString)

reg_exp = "NP: {<DT>?<JJ>*<NN>}"
rp = nltk.RegexpParser(reg_exp)
output = rp.parse(output.tags)
print(output.draw())
```

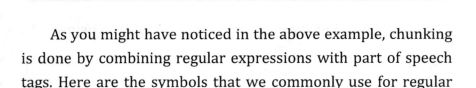

As you might have noticed in the above example, chunking
is done by combining regular expressions with part of speech
tags. Here are the symbols that we commonly use for regular
expressions:

- + = to match 1 or more
- ? = to match 0 or 1 repetitions.
- = to match 0 or MORE repetitions
- . = to match any character except a new line

To denote the part of speech tags, we use < and >, and
regular expressions can be added within these tags themselves.
Let us give another example using the corpus:

```
import nltk
```

```
from nltk.corpus import state_union
from nltk.tokenize import PunktSentenceTokenizer

nltk.download('state_union')
train = state_union.raw("2005-GWBush.txt")
sample = state_union.raw("2006-GWBush.txt")

custom_sent_tokenizer =
PunktSentenceTokenizer(train)

tokenized =
custom_sent_tokenizer.tokenize(sample)

def process_text():
    try:
        for x in tokenized:
            words = nltk.word_tokenize(x)
            tagged = nltk.pos_tag(words)
            chunkGram = r"""Chunk:
{<RB.?>*<VB.?>*<NNP>+<NN>?}"""
            chunkParser =
nltk.RegexpParser(chunkGram)
            chunked = chunkParser.parse(tagged)
            chunked.draw()

    except Exception as ex:
        print(str(ex))

print(process_text())
```

The code will return a parse tree.

Here is the main line for the above code:

```
chunkGram = r"""Chunk:
{<RB.?>*<VB.?>*<NNP>+<NN>?}"""
```

The line can be broken down as follows:

- `<RB.?>*` = "0 or more of any tense of the adverb," followed by:

- `<VB.?>*` = "0 or more of any tense of the verb," followed by:

- <NNP>+ = "One or more proper nouns," followed by
- <NN>? = "zero or one singular noun."

We may be in need of accessing the data via our program. In this case, the **"chunked"** variable is an NLTK tree. Every "chunk" and **"non-chunk"** should be a sub tree of the tree. To reference these, we can use **chunked.subtrees**. We can then be able to iterate over the subtrees as shown below:

```
for subtree in chunked.subtrees():
                print(subtree)
```

Our interest may only be to get the chunks and ignore the rest. To get these, we can use the filter parameter in the **chunked.subtrees()** call as demonstrated below:

```
for subtree in chunked.subtrees(filter=lambda t:
t.label() == 'Chunk'):
                print(subtree)
```

In the above case, we have done filtering so as to show the subtrees with a label of Chunk. At this point, you should have the following as the complete code:

```
import nltk
from nltk.corpus import state_union
from nltk.tokenize import PunktSentenceTokenizer

train = state_union.raw("2005-GWBush.txt")
sample = state_union.raw("2006-GWBush.txt")

custom_sent_tokenizer =
PunktSentenceTokenizer(train)

tokenized =
custom_sent_tokenizer.tokenize(sample)
```

```python
def process_text():
    try:
        for x in tokenized:
            words = nltk.word_tokenize(x)
            tagged = nltk.pos_tag(words)
            chunkGram = r"""Chunk:
{<RB.?>*<VB.?>*<NNP>+<NN>?}"""
            chunkParser =
nltk.RegexpParser(chunkGram)
            chunked = chunkParser.parse(tagged)

            print(chunked)
            for subtree in
chunked.subtrees(filter=lambda t: t.label() ==
'Chunk'):
                print(subtree)

            chunked.draw()

    except Exception as ex:
        print(str(ex))

process_text()
```

Other than the parse tree, the code will also return the following:

```
(S
  (Chunk PRESIDENT/NNP GEORGE/NNP W./NNP
BUSH/NNP)
  'S/POS
  (Chunk ADDRESS/NNP)
  BEFORE/IN
  (Chunk A/NNP JOINT/NNP SESSION/NNP)
  OF/IN
  (Chunk THE/NNP CONGRESS/NNP ON/NNP THE/NNP
STATE/NNP)
  OF/IN
  (Chunk THE/NNP UNION/NNP January/NNP)
  31/CD
  ,/,
  2006/CD
```

```
(Chunk THE/NNP PRESIDENT/NNP)
:/:
(Chunk Thank/NNP)
you/PRP
all/DT
./.)
(Chunk PRESIDENT/NNP GEORGE/NNP W./NNP BUSH/NNP)
(Chunk ADDRESS/NNP)
(Chunk A/NNP JOINT/NNP SESSION/NNP)
(Chunk THE/NNP CONGRESS/NNP ON/NNP THE/NNP
STATE/NNP)
(Chunk THE/NNP UNION/NNP January/NNP)
(Chunk THE/NNP PRESIDENT/NNP)
(Chunk Thank/NNP)
```

Chinking

Once you are done with chunking your text, you may
realize that the chunks that you get still have some text that
you don't like. You may lack an idea about how to remove them
through chunking. In such a case, chinking is the solution.

Chinking is simply a process that you use to remove a
chunk from a chunk. The chunk that is removed from the
chunk is referred to as the chink.

Remember that in our code, we denoted the chunks using
{}. To denote the chinks, we use }{ in the regular expression
part.

Let us use the same code but specify this:

```
import nltk
from nltk.corpus import state_union
from nltk.tokenize import PunktSentenceTokenizer

train = state_union.raw("2005-GWBush.txt")
```

```
sample = state_union.raw("2006-GWBush.txt")

custom_sent_tokenizer =
PunktSentenceTokenizer(train)

tokenized =
custom_sent_tokenizer.tokenize(sample)

def process_text():
    try:
        for x in tokenized:
            words = nltk.word_tokenize(x)
            tagged = nltk.pos_tag(words)
            chunkGram = r"""Chunk: {<.*>+}
}<VB.?|IN|DT|TO>+{"""
            chunkParser =
nltk.RegexpParser(chunkGram)
            chunked = chunkParser.parse(tagged)

            print(chunked)
            for subtree in
chunked.subtrees(filter=lambda t: t.label() ==
'Chunk'):
                print(subtree)

            chunked.draw()

    except Exception as ex:
        print(str(ex))

process_text()
```

The main logic for the code is in the following line:

```
chunkGram = r"""Chunk: {<.*>+}
}<VB.?|IN|DT|TO>+{"""
```

7-Social Media Mining

Social media is a great source of data. This data can be processed to get information. This information is knowledge and good for decision making. Social media is now a great source of customer opinions. These opinions provide businesses with a huge amount of data which they can analyze. By use of machine learning, businesses are able to extract such opinions in the form of text or audio and analyze them to determine the emotions behind them. If you have a product to sell, then opinion analysis is the best option for you.

Twitter is an example of a social media platform where users share short messages known as tweets. There are various ways through which individuals can share content on Twitter, including through text, pictures, and videos. With 500 million tweets made every day, we are presented with a lot of data that we can analyze. In this chapter, you will learn how to analyze Twitter data in Python.

Register your App

To be able to access Twitter data programmatically, you have to create an app that will be interacting with the Twitter API. To register this app, open the following URL on your browser:

http://apps.twitter.com

Sign in to your Twitter account and create a new application. They should give you a consumer key and a consumer secret. These are settings for the application that you have just created. You need to keep them private.

When you open the configuration page of the app, you will be able to request an access token and an access secret token. These should also be kept private since they will grant your application access to your Twitter account.

By default, the app is needed read-only permission, and this is all for this task. If you need your app to be granted write permissions on your Twitter account, you have to apply for new permission and Twitter requires you to negotiate for a new access token.

Accessing Twitter Data

There are various REST APIs provided by Twitter that we can use to interact with their various services. There are also many Python-based clients that we can use to work with Twitter services. Tweepy is one of them and it's what we will be using in this chapter. You can install it by running the following command:

For us to allow the Twitter app to access our Twitter

account on our behalf, we will use the OAuth interface. Just run
the following code for this:

```python
import tweepy
from tweepy import OAuthHandler

consumer_key = 'YOUR-CONSUMER-KEY'
consumer_secret = 'YOUR-CONSUMER-SECRET'
access_token = 'YOUR-ACCESS-TOKEN'
access_secret = 'YOUR-ACCESS-SECRET'

auth = OAuthHandler(consumer_key,
consumer_secret)
auth.set_access_token(access_token,
access_secret)

api = tweepy.API(auth)
```

We have made all the necessary importations and created
a number of variables. You have to enter the correct keys, that
is, the ones you received after creating your Twitter app. Flor
example, to read our own timelime, we can run the following
code:

```python
for status in
tweepy.Cursor(api.home_timeline).items(10):
    # Processing a single status
    print(status.text)
```

In the above code, we are only trying to access 10 tweets.
However, it is possible for us to access and read more tweets
than this. We have also created a variable named status which
is an instance of the **Status()** class, which is a nice wrapper for
accessing the data. The JSON response obtained from the
Twitter API can be found at the attribute **_json** which is a

---

dictionary rather than a raw **JSON string**.

The above code can be rewritten as follows to store/process JSON data:

```python
for status in
tweepy.Cursor(api.home_timeline).items(10):
    # Processing a single status
    process_or_store(status._json)
```

To get the list of all the account followers, we can use the following code:

```python
for friend in tweepy.Cursor(api.friends).items():
    process_or_store(friend._json)
```

To get the list of all the tweets, we can run the following code:

```python
for tweet in
tweepy.Cursor(api.user_timeline).items():
    process_or_store(tweet._json)
```

Notice the use of the **process_or_store() function** which is just a placeholder for custom implementation. To make it simple, you can choose to print out JSON, a line at a time as follows:

```python
def process_or_store(tweet):
    print(json.dumps(tweet))
```

Streaming

We may be in need of maintaining an open connection and keep on collecting all the incoming tweets. This is the best scenario for us to use the streaming API. There is a need for us to extend the **StreamListener()** to customize the way we process incoming data. Let us create an example that demonstrates how to collect all the incoming tweets under a certain hash tag:

```python
from tweepy import Stream
from tweepy.streaming import StreamListener

class MyListener(StreamListener):

    def on_data(self, data):
        try:
            with open('python.json', 'a') as f:
                f.write(data)
                return True
        except BaseException as e:
            print("Error on_data: %s" % str(e))
        return True

    def on_error(self, status):
        print(status)
        return True

twitter_stream = Stream(auth, MyListener())
twitter_stream.filter(track=['#python'])
```

It is possible for us to collect tons of tweets within a minute depending on the search term that we are using. This is very true when we have a live event that covers the world.

Text Pre-Processing

At this point, you know how to collect data from Twitter. In this section, we will be exploring the structure of a tweet before we dig into the processing step.

Now you have collected your tweets and stored them in the form of JSON. The following code can help us to analyze the structure of a tweet:

```python
import json

with open('mytweets.json', 'r') as f:
    line = f.readline() # to read the first
tweet/line only
    tweet = json.loads(line) # load the tweet as
Python dict
    print(json.dumps(tweet, indent=4)) # a
pretty-print
```

Here are the key attributes of a tweet:
- text- the tweet text itself
- created_at- the date the tweet was created
- favorite_count, retweet_count- the number of retweets and favourites.
- favorited, retweeted- boolean that states whether the authenticated user has favourited or retweeted the tweet.
- lang- an acronym for the language such as "en" for English.
- id- a tweet identifier
- place, coordinates, geo- the geo-location information if it's available
- user- the full profile of the author
- entities- list of entities like URLs, @-mentions, hashtags, and symbols
- in_reply_to_user_id- the user identifier if the tweet is a reply to a certain user
- in_reply_to_status_id- the status identifier in case the tweet is a reply to a status

Above we have a lot of information that we can play around with.

Tokenizing a Tweet Text

We have already used the nltk library for tokenizing our text. We can also use the same library to tokenize our tweet text. This is demonstrated below:

```
from nltk.tokenize import word_tokenize

tweet = 'RT @nic123: This is an example! :C
http://example.com #NLP'
print(word_tokenize(tweet))
```

It should print the following output:

```
['RT', '@', 'nic123', ':', 'This', 'is', 'an',
'example', '!', ':', 'C', 'http', ':',
'//example.com', '#', 'NLP']
```

You will realize that there are some parameters that the regular English tokenizer does not capture. Here is the code that demonstrates how these can be captured:

```
import re
from nltk.tokenize import word_tokenize

emoticons_str = r"""
    (?:
        [:=;] # Eyes
        [oO\-]? # Nose)
        [D\)\]\(\]/\\OpP] # Mouth
    )"""

regex_str = [
```

```
    emoticons_str,
    r'<[^>]+>', # HTML tags
    r'(?:@[\w_]+)', # @-mentions
    r"(?:\#+[\w_]+[\w\'_\-]*[\w_]+)", # hash-tags
    r'http[s]?://(?:[a-z]|[0-9]|[$-
_@.&amp;+]|[!*\(\),]|(?:%[0-9a-f][0-9a-f]))+', #
URLs

    r'(?:(?:\d+,?)+(?:\.?\d+)?)', # numbers
    r"(?:[a-z][a-z'\-_]+[a-z])", # words with -
and '
    r'(?:[\w_]+)', # other words
    r'(?:\S)' # any other thing
]

tokens_re =
re.compile(r'('+'|'.join(regex_str)+')',
re.VERBOSE | re.IGNORECASE)
emoticon_re = re.compile(r'^'+emoticons_str+'$',
re.VERBOSE | re.IGNORECASE)

def tokenize(s):
    return tokens_re.findall(s)

def preprocess(s, lowercase=False):
    tokens = tokenize(s)
    if lowercase:
        tokens = [token if
emoticon_re.search(token) else token.lower() for
token in tokens]
    return tokens

tweet = 'RT @nic123: This is an example! :C
http://example.com #NLP'
print(word_tokenize(tweet))
```

This will return the following output:

```
['RT', '@', 'nic123', ':', 'This', 'is', 'an',
'example', '!', ':', 'C', 'http', ':',
'//example.com', '#', 'NLP']
```

The above output shows that the various unique

parameters have been preserved as individual tokens.

To process all the tweets that were saved in a file, we can run the following code:

```
with open('mytweets.json', 'r') as f:
    for line in f:
        tweet = json.loads(line)
        tokens = preprocess(tweet['text'])
        do_something_else(tokens)
```

The tokenizer is not perfect, but it provides you with a general idea. We have used the idea of regular expressions to do the tokenization, and it is a common choice for such kinds of problems.

Term Frequencies

Now that we have collected the data and done some pre-processing on it, we are ready to perform some basic analysis on it. In this section, we will be analyzing the term frequencies and extract the meaningful terms from our tweets.

Suppose that we have already collected our tweets, the first analysis that we can perform is word count. We can check for the words that occur frequently in our dataset.

The custom tokenizer can help us in splitting our tweets into a list of terms. We will use the **preprocess() function** to capture the Twitter-specific aspects of text like @-mentions, #hashtags, URLs and emoticons. For us to be able to keep the frequencies during the processing of the tweets, we will use the **collection.Counter()** which is a dictionary that comes with various functions. Run the following code:

```
import json
import operator
from collections import import Counter

fname = 'mytweets.json'
with open(fname, 'r') as f:
    count_all = Counter()
    for line in f:
        tweet = json.loads(line)
        # Creating a list of the terms
        terms_all = [term for term in
preprocess(tweet['text'])]
        # Updating the counter
        count_all.update(terms_all)
    # Printing the top 5 frequent words
    print(count_all.most_common(5))
```

This will return stopwords as part of the top **5 words**. We need to remove these.

Removing Stopwords

We now need to remove all the words that don't have a significant meaning from our tweets. Some words that we will target include rt (for re-tweets) and via(for mentioning the original owner of an article). These are not part of the original stop-word list. We can handle them using the following code:

```
import string
from nltk.corpus import stopwords

punctuation = list(string.punctuation)
stop = stopwords.words('english') + punctuation +
['rt', 'via']
```

Now, the variable named terms_all in our first example can be substituted using a code such as the one given below:

```
terms_stop = [term for term in
preprocess(tweet['text']) if term not in stop]
```

You can now count the terms, sort them and print the top 5 most occurring words. You will realize that the list will change.

Other than removing the list of stop-words, it is possible for us to customize the list of tokens/words that we have interest in. The following code demonstrates this:

```
# Count the terms once
terms_single = set(terms_all)
# Count only the hashtags
terms_hash = [term for term in
preprocess(tweet['text'])
              if term.startswith('#')]
# Count only terms, no mentions, no hashtags
terms_only = [term for term in
preprocess(tweet['text'])
              if term not in stop and
              not term.startswith(('#', '@'))]
```

8-NLTK for Sentiment Analysis

Since we discussed sentiment analysis previously, you know that it involves analyzing a set of text to classify it. The purpose of sentiment analysis is to classify text as either positive or negative. The classification task is normally done on two classes, positive and negative, but it is possible for us to add other classes or categories.

In the previous section, we used VADER for sentiment analysis. In this section, we will use NLTK for this.

Supervised Classification

When doing supervised text classification, the text is classified by use of labeled data. We will be using the **movie_reviews** corpus provided by the NLTK for this. This corpus comes with 2K move reviews together with sentiment polarity classification. We will be using two categories for classification purposes, negative and positive. The corpus comes with the reviews placed in these categories.

```python
from nltk.corpus import movie_reviews

# show all reviews
print (len(movie_reviews.fileids()))

# The Review categories
print (movie_reviews.categories())

# Total positive reviews
print (len(movie_reviews.fileids('pos')))

# Total negative reviews
print (len(movie_reviews.fileids('neg')))

positive_review_file =
movie_reviews.fileids('pos')[0]
print (positive_review_file)
```

The code should return the following result when executed:

```
2000
['neg', 'pos']
1000
1000
pos/cv000_29590.txt
```

We began by importing the corpus from **nltk.corpus**. We have then printed the total number of reviews by use of the **len() function**, and the above output tells us that there are a total of 2000 reviews.

We have then invoked the **categories()** to tell us the categories or classes into which the reviews have been placed.

The output tells us that there are two categories, **neg** and **pos** for negative and positive categories respectively.

We have again used the **len() function** to know the total number of positive reviews as well as the total number of negative reviews. Each of these categories has 1000 reviews.

The positive reviews will be kept in the *.txt* file shown in the output.

Creating a List of Movie Review Document

We will create a list with an array of tuples of all movie review words and their categories, that is, pos or neg. modify the code to the following:

```
from nltk.corpus import movie_reviews
from random import shuffle

positive_review_file =
movie_reviews.fileids('pos')[0]

documents = []

for category in movie_reviews.categories():
    for fileid in
movie_reviews.fileids(category):

documents.append((movie_reviews.words(fileid),
category))

print (len(documents))

print (documents[0])
  # shuffle the list of document
shuffle(documents)
```

Notice that we have imported the **shuffle() function** from the **random library**. We have then used the function to shuffle the documents. The code should return the following output:

```
2000
(['plot', ':', 'two', 'teen', 'couples', 'go', 'to', ...], 'neg')
```

Feature Extraction

We should define criteria that will help us in classifying text into either of the categories. Based on the criteria, the classifier will be able to tell the category into which a particular text falls. The criteria are known as a feature. It is possible for us to use more than one feature to train our classifier.

In our example, we will be using the top-N words feature. We will first fetch all the words contained in the **movie_reviews** database and create a list out of it:

```
all_words = [word.lower() for word in
movie_reviews.words()]

# print the first 10 words
print (all_words[:10])
```

The code will return the following list of words:

```
['plot', ':', 'two', 'teen', 'couples', 'go', 'to', 'a', 'church', 'party']
```

Create a Frequency

Distribution

The purpose of a frequency distribution is to create the number of times that every word occurs in the whole list of words.

First, import the FreqDist function from the **nltk library**:

```
from nltk import FreqDist
```

Next, add the following code:

```
all_words_frequency = FreqDist(all_words)
 print (all_words_frequency)

# show the 10 most frequently occurring words
print (all_words_frequency.most_common(10))
```

The code should return the following result:

```
<FreqDist with 39768 samples and 1583820 outcomes>
[(',', 77717), ('the', 76529), ('.', 65876), ('a', 38106), ('and', 35576), ('of'
, 34123), ('to', 31937), ('"', 30585), ('is', 25195), ('in', 21822)]
```

We have shown the 10 most frequently occurring words.

Remove Punctuation and Stopwords

From the list of top 10 most occurring words shown above, it is very clear that the words that occur most are either **stopwords** or **punctuation marks**.

Stopwords are the words used frequently in the text but they carry no significant meaning when it comes to text analysis. Examples of such words include **I, me, the, a, my, and, is, he, she, are, we,** etc.

Punctuation marks such as full stop and comma occur frequently in the text but they carry no significant meaning when it comes to text analysis.

Let us clean the data by removing stopwords and punctuation marks.

First, import the stopwords function from **nltk.corpus**:

```
from nltk.corpus import stopwords
```

Now, run the following code:

```
stopwords_english = stopwords.words('english')
print (stopwords_english)
```

This should return the list of all stopwords found in the text:

```
['i', 'me', 'my', 'myself', 'we', 'our', 'ours',
'ourselves', 'you', "you're", "you've", "you'll",
"you'd", 'your', 'yours', 'yourself',
'yourselves', 'he', 'him', 'his', 'himself',
'she', "she's", 'her', 'hers', 'herself', 'it',
"it's", 'its', 'itself', 'they', 'them', 'their',
'theirs', 'themselves', 'what', 'which', 'who',
'whom', 'this', 'that', "that'll", 'these',
'those', 'am', 'is', 'are', 'was', 'were', 'be',
'been', 'being', 'have', 'has', 'had', 'having',
'do', 'does', 'did', 'doing', 'a', 'an', 'the',
'and', 'but', 'if', 'or', 'because', 'as',
'until', 'while', 'of', 'at', 'by', 'for',
'with', 'about', 'against', 'between', 'into',
'through', 'during', 'before', 'after', 'above',
'below', 'to', 'from', 'up', 'down', 'in', 'out',
'on', 'off', 'over', 'under', 'again', 'further',
'then', 'once', 'here', 'there', 'when', 'where',
```

```
'why', 'how', 'all', 'any', 'both', 'each',
'few', 'more', 'most', 'other', 'some', 'such',
'no', 'nor', 'not', 'only', 'own', 'same', 'so',
'than', 'too', 'very', 's', 't', 'can', 'will',
'just', 'don', "don't", 'should', "should've",
'now', 'd', 'll', 'm', 'o', 're', 've', 'y',
'ain', 'aren', "aren't", 'couldn', "couldn't",
'didn', "didn't", 'doesn', "doesn't", 'hadn',
"hadn't", 'hasn', "hasn't", 'haven', "haven't",
'isn', "isn't", 'ma', 'mightn', "mightn't",
'mustn', "mustn't", 'needn', "needn't", 'shan',
"shan't", 'shouldn', "shouldn't", 'wasn',
"wasn't", 'weren', "weren't", 'won', "won't",
'wouldn', "wouldn't"]
```

We can now create a new list of words but remove the stopwords. Run the following code:

```
all_words_without_stopwords = [word for word in
all_words if word not in stopwords_english]

# print all the first 10 words
print (all_words_without_stopwords[:10])
```

It now returns the following result:

```
['plot', ':', 'two', 'teen', 'couples', 'go',
'church', 'party', ',', 'drink']
```

You can see that the list of the top 10 most occurring words has changed. This is because stopwords have been removed from the list.

Now that we have removed the stopwords, we need to go ahead and remove the punctuation. We will use the **string library** for this. Run the following code to perform the removal of the punctuation marks:

```
import string
 print (string.punctuation)
```

```
# create a new words list by removing
punctuation from all_words
all_words_without_punctuation = [word for word in
all_words if word not in string.punctuation]

# to print the top 10 words
print (all_words_without_punctuation[:10])
```

What we have done is that we have removed the punctuation marks from the list named **all_words**. Punctuation marks like semicolon and the fullstop have been removed as shown in the output given below:

```
!"#$%&'()*+,-./:;<=>?@[\]^_`{|}~
['plot', 'two', 'teen', 'couples', 'go', 'to', 'a', 'church', 'party', 'drink']
```

Removing both Stopwords and Punctuation

In the previous example, we started by removing the stopwords then we moved to remove the punctuation. Note that each was done at its own time. The code given below can help us to remove both the stopwords and the punctuation from the **all_words** list:

```
import string
stopwords_english = stopwords.words('english')

all_words_clean = []
for word in all_words:
    if word not in stopwords_english and word not
in string.punctuation:
        all_words_clean.append(word)
```

```
print (all_words_clean[:10])
```

The code should return the following result upon execution:

```
['plot', 'two', 'teen', 'couples', 'go', 'church', 'party', 'drink', 'drive', 'g
et']
```

We have created a new list and given it the name **all_words_clean**. We have then cleaned the text from stopwords and punctuation.

Frequency Distribution of the cleaned words list

Now that we have removed stopwords and punctuation, we can get the frequency distribution of the new list. The following code can help us get this:

```
all_words_frequency = FreqDist(all_words_clean)

print (all_words_frequency)

# print the top 10 most frequently occurring
words
print (all_words_frequency.most_common(10))
```

The code should return the following output:

```
<FreqDist with 39586 samples and 710578 outcomes>
[('film', 9517), ('one', 5852), ('movie', 5771), ('like', 3690), ('even', 2565),
('time', 2411), ('good', 2411), ('story', 2169), ('would', 2109), ('much', 2049
)]
```

See that we simply invoked the FreqDist function and passed the name of the list of it. Before we removed the stopwords and punctuation, we had the frequency distribution as follows:

```
<FreqDist with 39768 samples and 1583820 outcomes>
```

After removing the stopwords and punctuation, it has changed to the following:

```
<FreqDist with 39586 samples and 710578 outcomes>
```

The above shows that a significant change has occurred in terms of change in the number of words. We also have the top 10 most occurring words and their frequency, which is the number of times they occur to the text. After removing the stopwords and punctuation, you can tell that this list has some more meaningful words.

Create a Word Feature by use of 2000 most frequently occurring words

We now need to use the 2000 most occurring words as our feature. Let us first print the frequency of all the words:

```
print (len(all_words_frequency))
```

This should return the following:

```
>>> print (len(all_words_frequency))
39586
>>>
```

Let us try to get the 2000 most occurring words and access 10 of them:

```
most_common_words =
all_words_frequency.most_common(2000)
print (most_common_words[:10])
```

This returns the following:

```
>>> most_common_words = all_words_frequency.most_common(2000)
>>> print (most_common_words[:10])
[('film', 9517), ('one', 5852), ('movie', 5771), ('like', 3690), ('even', 2565),
 ('good', 2411), ('time', 2411), ('story', 2169), ('would', 2109), ('much', 2049
)]
>>>
```

Let us print the most common words:

```
print (most_common_words[1990:])
```

This should return the following:

```
>>> print (most_common_words[1990:])
[('bound', 64), ('asking', 64), ('remain', 64), ('niro', 64), ('naturally', 64),
 ('aware', 64), ('regular', 64), ('international', 64), ('anna', 64), ('exact',
64)]
>>>
```

The most common elements of the list are tuples. Let us get only the first element of each tuple of our word list:

```
word_features = [item[0] for item in
most_common_words]
print (word_features[:10])
```

This should return the following:

```
>>> word_features = [item[0] for item in most_common_words]
>>> print (word_features[:10])
['film', 'one', 'movie', 'like', 'even', 'good', 'time', 'story', 'would', 'much
']
>>>
```

Create a Feature Set

We can come up with a function that we can use to create a feature set. We will then use the feature set for training our classifier.

We need to create a feature extractor function that will be checking whether the words contained in a particular document are available in the **word_features** list or not. The following code demonstrates how to do this:

```
def document_features(document):
    # make the function to remove
repeated/duplicate tokens in a list
    document_words = set(document)
    features = {}
    for word in word_features:
        features['contains(%s)' % word] = (word
in document_words)
    return features

# get the first file with negative movie reviews
movie_review_file =
movie_reviews.fileids('neg')[0]
print (movie_review_file)
```

This should return the following result:

> neg/cv000_29416.txt

Remember that we had created a **documents** list which has data onto all the movie reviews. It has elements in the form of tuples and word list is the first element and review category is the second item in the tuple. Let us now print the first tuple of the document list:.

```
print (documents[0])
```

```
>>> print (documents[0])
(['retelling', 'the', 'classic', 'story', 'of', 'joan', ...], 'neg')
>>>
```

We can now loop through our documents list to create a feature set list by use of the **document_features function** that we have defined above.

Every item in the **feature_set** will be a tuple. The first item in the tuple will be the dictionary returned from the above function.

The second item of the tuple will be the category of the movie review, which is **pos** or **neg.**

```
feature_set = [(document_features(doc), category)
for (doc, category) in documents]
print (feature_set[0])
```

Here is a section of the received output:

```
({'contains(book)': False, 'contains(jack)':
False, 'contains(giant)': False,
'contains(bruce)': False, 'contains(easily)':
False, 'contains(ii)': True, 'contains(studio)':
False, 'contains(project)': False,
'contains(voice)': False, 'contains(issues)':
True, 'contains(angel)': False,
'contains(cliche)': False, 'contains(lucky)':
False, 'contains(tale)': False,
'contains(jonathan)': False, 'contains(saying)':
```

False, 'contains(fame)': False,
'contains(seconds)': False, 'contains(key)':
False, 'contains(others)': False,
'contains(age)': False, 'contains(filmed)':
False, 'contains(case)': True, 'contains(young)':
True, 'contains(viewer)': False,
'contains(meant)': False, 'contains(pass)':
False, 'contains(attempt)': False,
'contains(gold)': False, 'contains(kill)': False,
'contains(become)': False, 'contains(killing)':
False, 'contains(teacher)': False,
'contains(laughing)': False, 'contains(serial)':
False, 'contains(spectacular)': False,
'contains(material)': False, 'contains(took)':
False, 'contains(short)': True,
'contains(jones)': False, 'contains(window)':
False, 'contains(creative)': False,
'contains(product)': False, 'contains(thus)':
True, 'contains(humor)': False,
'contains(straight)': False, 'contains(kind)':
False, 'contains(haunting)': False,
'contains(gun)': False, 'contains(dollars)':
False, 'contains(shoot)': False,
'contains(search)': False, 'contains(welcome)':
False, 'contains(possibly)': True,
'contains(willis)': False, 'contains(joe)':
False, 'contains(plot)': True,
'contains(otherwise)': False, 'contains(taking)':
False, 'contains(knows)': False,
'contains(stand)': False,
'contains(appropriate)': False,
'contains(track)': False, 'contains(liners)':
False, 'contains(hearted)': False,
'contains(likable)': False, 'contains(tragedy)':
False, 'contains(clooney)': False,
'contains(credit)': False,
'contains(atmosphere)': False,
'contains(across)': False, 'contains(level)':
False, 'contains(decision)': False,
'contains(babe)': False, 'contains(blame)':
False, 'contains(90)': False, 'contains(nudity)':
False, 'contains(forward)': False,
'contains(real)': True, 'contains(sandler)':

False, 'contains(chance)': False,
'contains(development)': False,
'contains(slasher)': False, 'contains(avoid)':
False, 'contains(following)': False,
'contains(aliens)': False, 'contains(late)':
False, 'contains(best)': True, 'contains(style)':
False, 'contains(walter)': False,
'contains(grow)': False, 'contains(leave)':
False, 'contains(fiction)': False,
'contains(appealing)': False, 'contains(things)':
True, 'contains(laughs)': False,
'contains(events)': True, 'contains(drama)':
False, 'contains(social)': False,
'contains(need)': False, 'contains(mention)':
False, 'contains(epic)':

Training the Classifier

From the feature set that we have created above, we can come up with a different training set and separate **training/validation** set. We will use the training set to train our classifier and the validation set to test how accurate our classifier classifies our text.

Our first step is to create both the training and the validation datasets. We will be using the first **400** items in the feature set array as the test set while the rest of the data will be used as the train set. In most cases, we use **80%** of the data as the training set and **20%** of the data as the test set.

The splitting can be done by running the following code:

```
print (len(feature_set))

test_set = feature_set[:400]
train_set = feature_set[400:]
```

```
print (len(train_set))
print (len(test_set))
```

We have started by printing the length of the **feature_set.**
We have split the data onto test_set for testing and train_set for
training. We have then printed them on the console. The code
should return the following result:

```
2000
1600
400
```

Training the Classifier

We now need to use the training set to train our classifier. The
nltk library provides us with different types of classifiers such
as Naive Bayes Classifier, Decision Tree Classifier, Maximum
Entropy Classifier, Support Vector Machine Classifier, etc. In
our case, we will use the Naive Bayes Classifier. This is a
classifier which is easy to create and exhibits a nice
performance when dealing with small datasets. The classifier is
probabilistic and it relies on the Bayes ' theorem. Let us first
import this classifier from the nltk library:.

```
from nltk import NaiveBayesClassifier
```

Now, run the following code:

```
classifier =
NaiveBayesClassifier.train(train_set)
```

We have passed our training dataset to the classifier and assigned this to the classifier variable. This will train the classifier.

Testing the Classifier

We need to test the classifier to know its accuracy percentage. Note that the accuracy percentage will be changing each time that you run the code since the names array will be shuffled. First, let us import the classify function from the nltk library. This function will help us perform classification on our text:

```
from nltk import classify
```

Now, run the following code:

```
accuracy = classify.accuracy(classifier,
test_set)
print (accuracy)
```

We have created the variable accuracy which should store the accuracy percentage of our classifier. In my case, I got an accuracy of **0.7975**, which is equivalent to **79.75** percent.

Now that our classifier is ready, trained and tested, we can pass some custom review of it and see its performance:

```
from nltk.tokenize import word_tokenize
```

```python
custom_review = "I hated the restaurant. It was a disaster eating there. Poor services, arrogant waiters."
custom_review_tokens = word_tokenize(custom_review)
custom_review_set = document_features(custom_review_tokens)
print (classifier.classify(custom_review_set))

prob_result = classifier.prob_classify(custom_review_set)
print (prob_result)
print (prob_result.max())
print (prob_result.prob("neg"))
print (prob_result.prob("pos"))

custom_review = "It was a wonderful and amazing restaurant. I loved eating my meal there. Best services, hospitable waiters."
custom_review_tokens = word_tokenize(custom_review)
custom_review_set = document_features(custom_review_tokens)

print (classifier.classify(custom_review_set))

# probability result
prob_result = classifier.prob_classify(custom_review_set)
print (prob_result)
print (prob_result.max())
print (prob_result.prob("neg"))
print (prob_result.prob("pos"))
```

The code returns the following result:

```
neg
<ProbDist with 2 samples>
neg
0.9999994435482947
5.564517080291968e-07
neg
<ProbDist with 2 samples>
neg
0.9999916207934206
8.379206598897348e-06
```

We have first imported the **word_tokenize function**. We then created the **custom_review variable** and passed a custom user review of it. The review is negative and it was classified accurately as negative. After getting the probabilistic review of the above, we have created another review, this time a positive review and assigned it to the variable **custome_review**. Although the review is positive, the above output shows that it was classified as negative. This called for us to improve our feature set so that we may be able to get an accurate classification. Run the following command to see the most informative features:

```
print
(classifier.show_most_informative_features(10))
```

The code returns the following result when executed:

```
>>> print (classifier.show_most_informative_features(10))
Most Informative Features
    contains(outstanding) = True            pos : neg     =      8.8 : 1.0
    contains(wonderfully) = True            pos : neg     =      8.5 : 1.0
         contains(mulan) = True             pos : neg     =      7.6 : 1.0
        contains(poorly) = True             neg : pos     =      7.2 : 1.0
         contains(lame) = True              neg : pos     =      7.2 : 1.0
        contains(seagal) = True             neg : pos     =      7.1 : 1.0
     contains(ridiculous) = True            neg : pos     =      6.5 : 1.0
        contains(lucas) = True              pos : neg     =      6.4 : 1.0
        contains(damon) = True              pos : neg     =      6.1 : 1.0
        contains(wasted) = True             neg : pos     =      5.6 : 1.0
None
>>>
```

From the above output, we can tell that the word **outstanding** has been used **8.8** times more in the positive reviews than in the negative reviews. The word **poorly** has been used **7.2** times more in the negative reviews than in positive reviews. These ratios are also referred to as **likelihood ratios**. This means that a review of words such as **outstanding** and **wonderfully** is more likely to be classified as a positive review. Similarly, a review of the words poorly and **lame** is more likely to be classified as being negative.

9-SciKit-Learn for Text Classification

Text classification is the most popular natural language processing task. It involves placing some text to its right category. In this chapter, we will be discussing how to use scikit-learn for text classification in Python. Scikit-learn is a machine learning library for Python.

The scikit-learn library comes with a corpus named **news**, hence we will use this to demonstrate classification in this chapter. Let us begin by having a look at this database:

```
from sklearn.datasets import fetch_20newsgroups
news = fetch_20newsgroups(subset='all')

print(len(news.data))
# 18846

print(len(news.target_names))
```

```python
print(news.target_names)
# ['alt.atheism', 'comp.graphics', 'comp.os.ms-
windows.misc', 'comp.sys.ibm.pc.hardware',
'comp.sys.mac.hardware', 'comp.windows.x',
'misc.forsale', 'rec.autos', 'rec.motorcycles',
'rec.sport.baseball', 'rec.sport.hockey',
'sci.crypt', 'sci.electronics', 'sci.med',
'sci.space', 'soc.religion.christian',
'talk.politics.guns', 'talk.politics.mideast',
'talk.politics.misc', 'talk.religion.misc']

for text, num_label in zip(news.data[:10],
news.target[:10]):
    print('[%s]:\t\t "%s ..."' %
(news.target_names[num_label],

text[:100].split('\n')[0]))
```

The code should give you the following result:

```
Downloading 20news dataset. This may take a few minutes.
Downloading dataset from https://ndownloader.figshare.com/files/5975967 (14 MB)
18846
20
['alt.atheism', 'comp.graphics', 'comp.os.ms-windows.misc', 'comp.sys.ibm.pc.har
dware', 'comp.sys.mac.hardware', 'comp.windows.x', 'misc.forsale', 'rec.autos',
'rec.motorcycles', 'rec.sport.baseball', 'rec.sport.hockey', 'sci.crypt', 'sci.e
lectronics', 'sci.med', 'sci.space', 'soc.religion.christian', 'talk.politics.gu
ns', 'talk.politics.mideast', 'talk.politics.misc', 'talk.religion.misc']
[rec.sport.hockey]:               "From: Mamatha Devineni Ratnam <mr47+@andrew.cm
u.edu> ..."
[comp.sys.ibm.pc.hardware]:               "From: mblawson@midway.ecn.uoknor.edu (
Matthew B Lawson) ..."
[talk.politics.mideast]:               "From: hilmi-er@dsv.su.se (Hilmi Eren)
..."
[comp.sys.ibm.pc.hardware]:               "From: guyd@austin.ibm.com (Guy Dawson)
..."
[comp.sys.mac.hardware]:               "From: Alexander Samuel McDiarmid <am2o
+@andrew.cmu.edu> ..."
[sci.electronics]:               "From: tell@cs.unc.edu (Stephen Tell) ..."
[comp.sys.mac.hardware]:               "From: lpa8921@tamuts.tamu.edu (Louis P
aul Adams) ..."
[rec.sport.hockey]:               "From: dchhabra@stpl.ists.ca (Deepak Chhabra) .
.."
[rec.sport.hockey]:               "From: dchhabra@stpl.ists.ca (Deepak Chhabra) .
.."
[talk.religion.misc]:               "From: arromdee@jyusenkyou.cs.jhu.edu (Ken Arro
mdee) ..."
```

We began by importing the necessary function. After that,

we have fetched the dataset. We have printed on the terminal to show the length and the number of class of the dataset. The output shows that we are to deal with **18846** and we will be classifying them into **20** categories. Now you know the structure of our data. When training a model, trail and error are required. We now need to come up with a simple way of training our model and then we test or evaluate it against the test data. This means that we have to split our data onto train and test sets. We can achieve this by calling the **train_test_split () function** provided y scikit-learn. First, import the function by running the following command :

```
from sklearn.cross_validation import
train_test_split
```

Now, run the following code:

```
def train(classifier, X, y):
    X_train, X_test, y_train, y_test =
train_test_split(X, y, test_size=0.25,
random_state=33)

    classifier.fit(X_train, y_train)
    print("Accuracy: %s" %
classifier.score(X_test, y_test))
    return classifier
```

We have defined a function named **train**. We have then split the dataset into training and test size. **25%** of the data will be used as the test set while the rest will be used as the training set. We have then fitted a classifier on these two datasets. Again, we will create a **Multinomial Naive Bayes** classifier. This classifier is mostly used for classification purposes. For us to transform the text into a feature vector, we will be using specific feature extractors from **sklearn. Feature_extraction Text TfidfVectorizer** has an advantage in that it can emphasize on the most important words of a text. We can now begin to build the classifier. Import the following libraries.

```
from sklearn.naive_bayes import MultinomialNB
from sklearn.pipeline import Pipeline
from sklearn.feature_extraction.text import
TfidfVectorizer
```

Now run the following code:

```
trial1 = Pipeline([
    ('vectorizer', TfidfVectorizer()),
    ('classifier', MultinomialNB()),
])

train(trial1, news.data, news.target)
```

We are running the first training trial on our classifier. It returns the following:

```
Accuracy: 0.846349745331
```

The above shows that we have an accuracy of **84.63 percent**, which is not bad at the firsttrial. However, it is possible for us to make an improvement on this. Most people first think of ignoring insignificant words.

We will use the stopwords list provided by **nltk:**. First, import the stopwords function from **nltk. Corpus** :

```
from nltk.corpus import stopwords
```

You can then run the following code:

```
trial2 = Pipeline([
    ('vectorizer',
TfidfVectorizer(stop_words=stopwords.words('engli
sh'))),
    ('classifier', MultinomialNB()),
])

train(trial2, news.data, news.target)
```

We are doing a second trial of training but this time, we have removed the insignificant words. This returns the following:

```
Accuracy: 0.877758913413
```

We now have an accuracy of **87.78 percent**, up from **84.63 percent**. That is a great improvement. Now, let us attempt to play with the alpha parameter provided by the Naïve-Bayes classifier. Let us use this parameter but first set it to a low value:

```
trial3 = Pipeline([
    ('vectorizer',
TfidfVectorizer(stop_words=stopwords.words('engli
sh'))),
    ('classifier', MultinomialNB(alpha=0.05)),
])

train(trial3, news.data, news.target)
```

We have done our third trial, with the alpha parameter

being set to **0.05**. The code returns the following:

```
Accuracy: 0.910229202037
```

We now have an accuracy of **91 percent**. That is a major improvement. Let us now do away with words that appear less than **5 times** in the document collection:

```
trial4 = Pipeline([
    ('vectorizer',
TfidfVectorizer(stop_words=stopwords.words('engli
sh'),
                            min_df=5)),
    ('classifier', MultinomialNB(alpha=0.05)),
])

train(trial4, news.data, news.target)
```

Note the **min_df parameter** has been set to **5** and this helps us do away with words with a frequency of less than **5**. The code returns the following:

```
Accuracy: 0.902801358234
```

The accuracy is now **90.28 percent**. Shockingly, it has gone down! Although it hasn't harmed us much, it is not useful for us at this point. Let us try something else that is more radical. We will now use the nltk tokenize to split our text into words then we use a stemmed to bring the words with their base form. Punctuations will be ignored since the **word_tokenize function** does not filter them out. Let's first make the following imports:

```
import string
from nltk.stem import PorterStemmer
```

```
from nltk import word_tokenize
```

Now, run the following code:

```
trial5 = Pipeline([
    ('vectorizer',
TfidfVectorizer(tokenizer=stemming_tokenizer,

stop_words=stopwords.words('english') +
list(string.punctuation))),
    ('classifier', MultinomialNB(alpha=0.05)),
])

train(trial5, news.data, news.target)
```

Above, we have done out **5th trial**. This will show a slight improvement, but the speed will go down completely. It will take the code a long time to run and return the results to you. The code will return the following result after long processing:

```
Accuracy: 0.911078098472
```

You have now learned how to use scikit-learn for text classification. It is a powerful machine learning library provided by Python.

10-Work with PDF files in Python

During your natural language processing tasks, you will normally want to process text data. This text data may be stored in PDF files. It is not much easy for one to extract data from PDF files since PDF is a proprietary format provided by Adobe and it comes with some little tricks when it comes to the extraction of data for processing.

However, there is a way for us to achieve this in Python. Python comes with numerous libraries that we can use for various tasks. In this chapter, we will use a number of Python libraries for this. These include the following:

- PyPDF2- To convert simple PDF files into text readable by Python.
- textract- To convert non-trivial, scanned PDF files into text readable by Python.

These will be used together with the nltk library to

determine how we can process text stored in PDF files. Since you already have the nltk library installed, installed the other two libraries by running the following commands:

```
pip3 install PyPDF2
pip3 install textract
```

The above commands will install the libraries that are needed for you to be able to parse PDF files and extract keywords from them. To make this easy, ensure that you have kept the PDF file in the same directory as the script file.

Reading PDF files

Now, run the following commands to import the necessary libraries and functions:

```
import PyPDF2
import textract
from nltk.tokenize import word_tokenize
from nltk.corpus import stopwords
```

Now that the libraries have been imported, run the following code to help you in reading your PDF file:

```
filename = 'Lorem-Ipsum.pdf'
#open function will allow you to read the pdf
file
pdfFileObj = open(filename,'rb')
#The variable pdfReader is a readable object that
is to be parsed
pdfReader = PyPDF2.PdfFileReader(pdfFileObj)
#knowing the number of pages will help us to
parse through all pages
num_pages = pdfReader.numPages
```

```
count = 0
text = ""
#while loop for reading every page
while count < num_pages:
    pageObj = pdfReader.getPage(count)
    count +=1
    text += pageObj.extractText()
#The if statement will check whether the above
library has returned #words.
if text != "":
    text = text
#If the above is False, we run the OCR library
textract for converting scanned/image PDF files
into text
else:
    text = textract.process(fileurl,
method='tesseract', language='eng')
```

Ensure that you specify the correct name for the PDF file in the **filename variable**. In my case, I am reading the **file Lorem-Ipsum.pdf** We have then invoked the **open() function** and passed the above variable to it to specify the file to be opened. The rb parameter specifies that the file will be opened for reading and the result will be stored in the **pdfFileObj variable**.

We have then invoked the **PyPDF2 library** to help us in doing the actual reading of the file. The while loop has been used for iterating through all the document pages. The value of the **count variable** will be incremented by **1** after every page read.

Now that the text has been read, we need to convert it into keywords. The following code can help you in doing this:

```
#using word_tokenize() function to break our text
phrases into its individual words
tokens = word_tokenize(text)
#creating a new list with punctuation that we
want to clean
```

```
punctuations = ['(',')',';',':','[',']',',']
#initializing the stopwords variable representin
a list of of words  that don't have much value as
keywords
stop_words = stopwords.words('english')
#Creating a list comprehension to return a list
of words which are NOT IN stop_words and NOT IN
punctuations.
keywords = [word for word in tokens if not word
in stop_words and not word in punctuations]
```

At this point, the keywords for the file are stored in a list. You can perform any operation you like with it. To have it remain searchable, keep it in a spreadsheet. You can also parse a number of files then perform a cluster analysis.

You should now have the following as the complete code:

```
pdfFileObj = open(filename,'rb')
#The variable pdfReader is a readable object that
is to be parsed
pdfReader = PyPDF2.PdfFileReader(pdfFileObj)
#knowing the number of pages will help us to
parse through all pages
num_pages = pdfReader.numPages
count = 0
text = ""
#while loop for reading every page
while count < num_pages:
    pageObj = pdfReader.getPage(count)
    count +=1
    text += pageObj.extractText()
#The if statement will check whether the above
library has returned #words.

if text != "":
    text = text
#If the above is False, we run the OCR library
textract for converting scanned/image PDF files
into text
else:
```

```
    text = textract.process(fileurl,
method='tesseract', language='eng')

#using word_tokenize() function to break our text
phrases into its individual words
tokens = word_tokenize(text)
#creating a new list with punctuation that we
want to clean
punctuations = ['(',')',';',':','[',']',',']
#initializing the stopwords variable representin
a list of of words  that don't have much value as
keywords
stop_words = stopwords.words('english')
#Creating a list comprehension to return a list
of words which are NOT IN stop_words and NOT IN
punctuations.
keywords = [word for word in tokens if not word
in stop_words and not word in punctuations]
print(keywords)
```

The code has read the file and returns the following result:

```
['Lorem', 'Ipsum', 'simply', 'dummy', 'text',
'printing', 'typesetting', 'industry', '.',
'Lorem', 'Ipsum', 'industry', "'s", 'standard',
'dummy', 'text', 'ever', 'since', '1500s',
'unknown', 'printer', 'took', 'galley', 'type',
'scrambled', 'make', 'type', 'specimen', 'book',
'.', 'It', 'survived', 'five', 'centuries',
'also', 'leap', 'electronic', 'typesetting',
'remaining', 'essentially', 'unchanged', '.',
'It', 'popularised', '1960s', 'release',
'Letraset', 'sheets', 'containing', 'Lorem',
'Ipsum', 'passages', 'recently', 'desktop',
'publishing', 'software', 'like', 'Aldus',
'PageMaker', 'including', 'versions', 'Lorem',
'Ipsum.It', 'long', 'established', 'fact',
'reader', 'distracted', 'readable', 'content',
'page', 'looking', 'layout', '.', 'The', 'point',
'using', 'Lorem', 'Ipsum', 'more-or-less',
'normal', 'distribution', 'letters', 'opposed',
'using', "'Content", 'content', "'", 'making',
```

'look', 'like', 'readable', 'English', '.',
'Many', 'desktop', 'publishing', 'packages',
'web', 'page', 'editors', 'use', 'Lorem',
'Ipsum', 'default', 'model', 'text', 'search',
"'lorem"', 'ipsum', "'"', 'uncover', 'many', 'web',
'sites', 'still', 'infancy', '.', 'Various',
'versions', 'evolved', 'years', 'sometimes',
'accident', 'sometimes', 'purpose', 'injected',
'humour', 'like', '.Contrary', 'popular',
'belief', 'Lorem', 'Ipsum', 'simply', 'random',
'text', '.', 'It', 'roots', 'pieceof',
'classical', 'Latin', 'literature', '45', 'BC',
'making', '2000', 'years', 'old', '.', 'Richard',
'McClintock', 'Latin', 'professor', 'Hampden-
Sydney', 'College', 'Virginia', 'looked', 'one',
'obscure', 'Latin', 'words', 'consectetur',
'Lorem', 'Ipsum', 'passage', 'going',
'throughthe', 'cites', 'word', 'classical',
'literature', 'discovered', 'undoubtable',
'source', '.', 'Lorem', 'Ipsum', 'comes',
'sections', '1.10.32', '1.10.33', '``', 'de',
'Finibus', 'Bonorum', 'et', 'Malorum', "'"',
'The', 'Extremes', 'Good', 'Evil', 'Cicero',
'written', '45', 'BC', '.', 'This', 'book',
'treatise', 'theory', 'ethics', 'popular',
'Renaissance', '.', 'The', 'first', 'line',
'Lorem', 'Ipsum', '``', 'Lorem', 'ipsum',
'dolor', 'sit', 'amet..', "'"', 'comes', 'line',
'section', '1.10.32.The', 'standard', 'chunk',
'Lorem', 'Ipsum', 'used', 'since', '1500s',
'reproduced', 'interested', '.', 'Sections',
'1.10.32', '1.10.33', '``', 'de', 'Finibus',
'Bonorum', 'et', 'Malorum', "'"', 'Cicero',
'also', 'reproduced', 'exact', 'original',
'form', 'accompanied', 'English', 'versions',
'1914', 'translation', 'H.', 'Rackham', '.']

The above output shows that the text was read from the file successfully.

Writing to PDF Files

Other than reading from a PDF file, you may want to write to it. With the PyPDF2 library, it is hard for you to directly write to a PDF file because of the font and other constraints. In this section, we will be demonstrating how to do that. We will be reading contents from a PDF file then we create a new PDF file and write the contents into the file.

First, run the following code to help in reading the contents of the first PDF document:

```python
import PyPDF2
mypdf = open('Lorem-Ipsum.pdf', mode='rb')
pdf_document = PyPDF2.PdfFileReader(mypdf)
pdf_document.numPages
page_one = pdf_document.getPage(0)
```

The above code will read the first page of our document. Our goal is to write the contents that have been read into a new PDF file. To do this, we can run the following script:

```python
pdf_document_writer = PyPDF2.PdfFileWriter()
```

In the above script, we have created an object that we can use to write to a PDF document. A page will first be added to the object and then we will pass the page that we have read from the previous document to it. The following script will help us achieve this:

```python
pdf_document_writer.addPage(page_one)
```

Next, we should open a new file using wb, that I, write binary permissions. When we open a file with such permissions, a new one will be created if it does not exist. Use the following script for this:

```
pdf_output_file = open('new_file.pdf', 'wb')
```

It is now time for us to call the **write() function** on our PDF writer object then we pass to it the newly created pdf file. Here is the script for this:

```
pdf_document_writer.write(pdf_output_file )
```

Ensure you have the following code:
```
import PyPDF2

mypdf = open('Lorem-Ipsum.pdf', mode='rb')
pdf_document = PyPDF2.PdfFileReader(mypdf)
pdf_document.numPages

page_one = pdf_document.getPage(0)

pdf_document_writer = PyPDF2.PdfFileWriter()

pdf_document_writer.addPage(page_one)

pdf_output_file = open('new_file.pdf', 'wb')

pdf_document_writer.write(pdf_output_file )
```

You can close your initial file and run the code. Move to the directory and find the **new_file.pdf file**. Open it to see its contents. It should have the contents of the first page of the previous file.

11-Work with Text Files in Python

Reading Text Files

When coding in Python, you will always want to read and write to files. We can use Python's **open() function** to open files for reading and writing. When this function is called, it normally returns a file object. The file object then comes with methods and attributes we can use to work with the file in question.

In this case, we will be reading a file named **colleagues.txt.** I will store it in the same directory as my Python script.

We can open it by running the following command:

```
myfile = open("colleagues.txt")
```

When you run the above code and no error is returned, just know that the file was opened successfully. We can now print the details of the file on the console by calling the **print function** as follows:

```
print(myfile)
```

The command will return the following on the console:

```
<_io.TextIOWrapper name='colleagues.txt' mode='r' encoding='cp1252'>
```

What the output tells us is that **myfile** is a wrapper to the **file colleagues.txt** and it will open the file in a read only mode.

If you get an error in the above process, you either provided a file name for a file that does not exist or you provided the wrong path to the file.

It is now time for us to see the contents of the file. We can do this by running the **read() function** on the **variable myfile**. The following code demonstrates how to do this:

```
myfile = open("colleagues.txt")
print(myfile.read())
```

The code prints the following upon execution:

```
nicholas john joel jeff mercy alice geoffrey cate catherine
```

Those are the contents of the file.

Now that we are done with the file, we should close it by calling the **close() method**. Again, you should call this method on the **myfile** object as shown below:

```
myfile.close()
```

In the above example, we have read the entire file at a go. However, it is possible for us to read our file line by line. This can be done by calling the **readlines () method** will return each line of the file in the form of a list item. The following code demonstrates how to do this:

```
myfile = open("colleagues.txt")
print(myfile.readlines())
```

I have changed the contents of the file **colleagues.txt** for each line to appear on its own line. The code returns the following upon execution:

```
['nicholas \n', 'john \n', 'joel \n', 'jeff \n', 'mercy \n', 'alice \n', 'geoffr
ey \n', 'cate \n', 'catherine\n']
```

In the above output, each line in the file is presented in the form of a list item.

Writing to Text Files

To write to a text file, we should open it with the **w** or **w+** permission. When you open the file in **w mode**, it will be opened for writing only. If you open the file in **w+ mode**, it will be opened for both reading and writing. If there is no file with the specified name, then a new one will be created. Note that when a file with contents is opened with the **w** or **w+** options, then its contents will be deleted and replaced with your new contents. The following code demonstrates this:

```
myfile = open("myfile.txt", 'w+')
print(myfile.read())
```

The above code should return nothing on the console since we have opened the file in **w+ mode** and all contents of the file have been removed. If you need to get an output, then you should append some text to this. This is what we are going to discuss below.

Now, we can call the **write() method** to write something into the file. The following code demonstrates this:

```
myfile = open("myfile.txt", 'w+')
print(myfile.read())
myfile.write("Text rerwitten to the file")
myfile.seek(0)
print(myfile.read())
```

In the above code, we have written some text into the file. The **seek() method** helps us to move the mouse cursor to the start of the file while the **read() method** helps us to read and display the contents of the new file on the console.

In most cases, you will not want to replace the original contents of the text file with the new contents but just to append text to it. This is possible in Python.

To append some content to a text file, you open the file with **a+ option**. This option opens the file for append plus read. The following code demonstrates how this can be done:

```
myfile = open("myfile.txt", 'a+')
myfile.seek(0)
print(myfile.read())
```

The code should return the contents of the file.

Next, you should append some contents to the file. The following code demonstrates how to do this:

```
myfile.write("\n New line appended to the file")
```

If you now read the contents of the file, you will realize that new contents have been added to it.

12-Word2Vec Algorithm

The Word2Vec algorithm helps us to come up with vector representations of words, also referred to as word embeddings. The vector of every word is a semantic representation that tells us how the word has been used in the context. This means that if there are two words used similarly in the text will have the same vector representations.

After mapping words into the vector space, you can use the vector maths to find the words with similar semantics.

Gensim provides us with a nice way of working with the Word2Vec algorithm. It is an open source library for Python used for natural language processing and it works very well with the NLTK corpus.

Install genism by running the following command:

```
pip3 install gensim
```

To learn the word embedding from a text, we should load and organize the text into sentences and provide them to the constructor of a new instance of Word2Vec(). The following code demonstrates this:

```
sentences = ...
model = Word2Vec(sentences)
```

Every sentence has to be tokenized. You can see the embedded vector of a certain word as follows:

```
print(model['word'])
```

Once you have trained a model, you can save it as follows:

```
model.wv.save_word2vec_format('model.bin')
```

You can also save the trained model in ASCII format by setting the parameter **binary** to **FALSE** as follows:

```
model.wv.save_word2vec_format('model.txt',
binary=False)
```

You can then load the model again as follows:

```
model = Word2Vec.load('model.bin')
```

The following code demonstrates this:

```
from gensim.models import Word2Vec
# defining the training data
sentences = [['here', 'is', 'our', 'first',
'sentence', 'for', 'algorithm'],
          ['this', 'is', 'our', 'second',
'sentence'],
          ['and', 'another', 'sentence'],
```

```
                ['and', 'more', 'sentence'],
                ['the', 'data', 'final', 'sentence']]
# training the model
model = Word2Vec(sentences, min_count=1)
# summarizing the loaded model
print(model)
# summarizing vocabulary
words = list(model.wv.vocab)
print(words)
# accessing vector for one word
print(model['sentence'])
# saving model
model.save('model.bin')
# loading model
new_model = Word2Vec.load('model.bin')
print(new_model)
```

The code returns the following result:

```
Word2Vec(vocab=15, size=100, alpha=0.025)
['the', 'is', 'second', 'for', 'algorithm',
'more', 'another', 'here', 'our', 'and', 'data',
'this', 'first', 'sentence', 'final']
[-0.00087532 -0.003146     0.00287502 -0.00309873
0.00371003  0.00337952
  0.00190806 -0.00364781 -0.00433836 -0.00121043
-0.00147259 -0.00165722
 -0.00175433  0.00112168 -0.00067589 -0.00398376
-0.00361586  0.00367874
  0.00461263  0.00327563  0.00066852  0.00229335
0.00310719 -0.00098965
  0.00228613 -0.00334832 -0.00289026  0.0027463
0.0024604   -0.00271762
  0.00035955  0.00280226 -0.00453688 -0.00425334
-0.00292284 -0.00499241
  0.00111463 -0.00151394 -0.00331069 -0.00016271
0.00240678  0.00012022
  0.00163469 -0.00379792  0.00052197 -0.0018658
0.00031518 -0.00167909
 -0.0043741   -0.00436597  0.00278581  0.00246136
-0.00173803 -0.00387167
 -0.00342849 -0.0026626   -0.00076751 -0.00037332
0.00165755  0.00430088
```

```
 -0.00097214  -0.00205026   0.00203719  -0.00352188
-0.00193794   0.00366378
  0.00052172   0.00434348   0.00423219  -0.00384075
-0.00496669   0.00245913
  0.00030505   0.00073599  -0.00265731   0.00074226
0.00237742   0.00419124
  0.00319323   0.00485818  -0.00485845  -0.00320383
0.00094171   0.00118153
  0.00304078  -0.00381625  -0.00226061  -0.00403162
-0.00201869   0.00465687
 -0.00389631  -0.00026738   0.00130404   0.00059255
-0.0041324    0.00196369
 -0.00247721   0.00383526  -0.00084784  -0.0033961 ]
```

That is how easy it is for one to create a word embedding with the Gensim library.

The following code shows how we can visualize the word vectors:

```python
from sklearn.decomposition import PCA
from gensim.models import Word2Vec
from matplotlib import pyplot
# defining the training data
sentences = [['here', 'is', 'our', 'first',
'sentence', 'for', 'algorithm'],
            ['this', 'is', 'our', 'second',
'sentence'],
            ['and', 'another', 'sentence'],
            ['and', 'more', 'sentence'],
            ['the', 'data', 'final', 'sentence']]
# training the model
model = Word2Vec(sentences, min_count=1)
# fitting a 2d PCA model to vectors
X = model[model.wv.vocab]
pca = PCA(n_components=2)
result = pca.fit_transform(X)
# creating a scatter plot for the projection
pyplot.scatter(result[:, 0], result[:, 1])
words = list(model.wv.vocab)
for i, word in enumerate(words):
    pyplot.annotate(word, xy=(result[i, 0],
result[i, 1]))
```

```
pyplot.show()
```

The code should return the following plot:

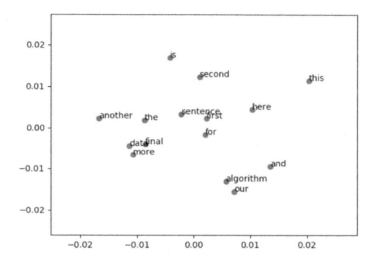

13-NLP Applications

NLP is everywhere even though we do not realize it. Consider the case where you attempt to send an email without the subject. It will prompt you to make corrections. This is natural language processing at work. Even though the use of NLP has been implemented in some areas, its implementation is expected to rise. Here are the areas in which NLP is currently applied:

Customer Service

Currently, there are many virtual assistance solutions that rely on the use of NLP. In these applications, the first request from the customer is handled by the AI. A good example is when a bank uses an automated system to answer customer queries or help them to know the best type of bank account they should go for. When the customer's queries become complex, the application will redirect to a helpline or to a right landing page. Nina is an example of such an application. Most banks have implemented it in their systems for customer support.

Market Intelligence

Most business markets are much impacted and influenced by market knowledge and information exchange amongst various companies, stakeholders, regulatory bodies and governments. Every business should stay updated with the current trends and changes in market standards. NLP is a great tool for monitoring market intelligence reports to extract new information that can help businesses to come up with new strategies.

When NLP is used in financial marketing, NLP can give great insights into the market status and employment changes, tender delays, closings and extracting information from repositories.

Management of Advertisement Funnel

You should know who your customer is, what they need and where they are located. NLP is a great tool to help you make sure that you do intelligent targeting when running your business ads. It will help you create the right ads, direct them to the right audience, the right place and at the right time. NLP has the feature of keyword matching that can help you to do this accurately.

Sentiment Analysis

NLP is one of the best tools through which businesses can analyze the feedback they get from their followers for the messages they publish on their social media platforms. With NLP, the emotion and attitude of the writer can be analyzed easily. The business can know the mood of the customers regarding their brand. This way, they can make any necessary changes to their products or services.

Such information is very important to make any necessary improvements. |They can also design a better customer experience.

Samuel Burns

Conclusion

This marks the end of this book. Natural Language processing is a branch of artificial intelligence that deals with machines such as computers interpreting natural languages such as English. This means that NLP has to deal with computers interacting with human languages.

Today, companies are generating too much data. This data is normally stored in the form of text. Due to the huge volume of the data, it may be hard for any business to process it manually. Thanks to natural language processing as it's the best tool to process such data. When processed, this data can give much knowledge which is of much importance to the business. Businesses can learn the passions and interests of their customers. This can help them adjust their plans appropriately so as to meet the demands of users.

With natural language processing, a computer can understand the human language while being spoken. This has led to the increased popularity of natural language processing, not forgetting the availability of big data, growing interest in machine-human communications and the discovery of new computing algorithms. With natural language processing, an intelligent system such as a robot can perform according to our instructions issued in a plain language such as English. NLP has been applied in various fields such as customer service, chatbots, market intelligence, managing advertisements, and sentiment analysis.

About the Author

Samuel Burns has a Ph.D. in Machine Learning and is an Artificial Intelligence developer, researcher, and educator as well as an Open Source Software developer. He has authored many papers as well as a number of popular software packages. Specialist in Data Mining and Security, Burns is an active machine learning researcher and regularly teaches courses and maintains resources for the data scientist.

Burn's research has pioneered developments in ensemble learning, outlier detection and profile discovery. He is involved in numerous international artificial intelligence and data mining research activities and conferences.

www.ingramcontent.com/pod-product-compliance
Lightning Source LLC
Chambersburg PA
CBHW071141050326
40690CB00008B/1523